Soundings

Also by Kennedy Warne

Roads Less Travelled: Twenty Years of Exploration with
    New Zealand Geographic. Penguin, 2008.
Let Them Eat Shrimp: The Tragic Disappearance of the
    Rainforests of the Sea. Island Press, 2011.
Tūhoe: Portrait of a Nation (with Peter James Quinn).
    Penguin, 2013.
View From the Road (with Arno Gasteiger). Penguin, 2014.
The Cuckoo and the Warbler: A True New Zealand Story
    (with Heather Hunt). Potton & Burton, 2016.
It's My Egg (And You Can't Have It!) (with Heather Hunt).
    Potton & Burton, 2017.

Soundings
Diving for stories in
the beckoning sea

Kennedy Warne

MASSEY UNIVERSITY PRESS

For Bronwyn

Loveliness unfathomable, as ever lover
saw in his young bride's eye! — Tell
me not of thy teeth-tiered sharks, and
thy kidnapping cannibal ways. Let
faith oust fact; let fancy oust memory;
I look deep down and do believe.

— Starbuck's reverie,
Herman Melville, *Moby-Dick*

Contents

Author's note

SOUNDINGS IS A MEMOIR of a life with the sea. It recounts my experiences partly above but mostly below the surface. I have been visiting and exploring the underwater world for 50 years. Much of this exploration has occurred on assignment for *National Geographic*. The chapters on South Africa, the Okavango Delta, Arabia, Kiribati and Tuvalu, the Philippines, harp seals and sharks expand on stories originally published in *National Geographic*. The introduction and part of the first chapter draw from pieces published in *New Zealand Geographic*.

My experiences among mangrove forests are not included in this book; they are the subject of my 2011 book *Let Them Eat Shrimp: The Tragic Disappearance of the Rainforests of the Sea*. Encounters with albatrosses and with New Zealand's marine reserves are also either absent or only glancingly referred to here, as they form chapters in my 2008 book *Roads Less Travelled: Twenty Years of Exploration with New Zealand Geographic*.

It is perhaps worth mentioning here that *New Zealand Geographic* and *National Geographic* are not related, other than by the generic word 'geographic' in their titles. (There is also an *Australian Geographic* and a *Canadian Geographic*.) It was my good fortune to co-found *New Zealand Geographic* in 1988 and to serve as the magazine's editor for 15 years. That experience taught me about writing, photography, design and production. In 1999, it opened the door to write for *National Geographic*. I have been writing for both magazines ever since.

Reflecting on the aquatic stories I have worked on over the past two decades brings pleasurable memories of people who helped make the research possible or who contributed their knowledge, skill and enthusiasm in the field. In South Africa, I think of Mark and Gail Addison, Charles Maxwell, Eric Simpson, Ryan Daly and Clare Keating, Peet Joubert, Lauren De Vos, Steve Benjamin and Jackie Sunde. In the Okavango Delta, Brad Bestelink, Andy Crawford, and Brad's father, PJ, come readily to mind. In the Seychelles, Michael Scholl, Rainer von Brandis and Nancy Bunbury. In Kuwait, Dareen Almojil. In Oman, Andy Wilson and Ahmed Salem. In Kiribati, Teweiariki Teaero and Claire Anterea. In New Zealand, Ruth and Lance Shaw and Bill Ballantine, who is rightly referred to as the father of New Zealand marine reserves.

For a marine education, I owe much to University of Auckland professors John Morton and Patricia Bergquist, freelance writer and naturalist John Walsby and my former cell biology lecturer Warren Judd. Warren later joined me as deputy editor of *New Zealand Geographic*, and took over as editor when I stepped down in 2004. Irrepressibly inquisitive about the natural world, he was my editorial collaborator from the magazine's very first issue.

For the journalistic pathway that created these opportunities, I thank John Woods, with whom I first started working in 1980 on the community newspaper he established in Thames, the *Hauraki Herald*. I learned my craft on the job. John and I launched *New Zealand Geographic* eight years later.

I value the opportunities I have had to work with *National Geographic* photographers over the past two decades: David Doubilet and Jennifer Hayes in South Africa, the Okavango Delta and the Philippines, Brian Skerry in the Gulf of St Lawrence and New Zealand, and Thomas Peschak in South Africa, the Seychelles and Arabia.

Among the editors I worked with at *National Geographic* are John Hoeffel, Lynn Addison and, for the longest time, Oliver Payne, who offered me my first assignment, and many to follow.

It was Tracey Borgfeldt, associate publisher at Massey University Press, who suggested I write this book. Our paths first crossed in 1995 when she shepherded to publication the large-format book *New Zealand Geographic*, showcasing photographs and stories from the first five years of *New Zealand Geographic* magazine. We stayed in touch, and the book you have in your hands has been brought to fruition by her, publisher Nicola Legat and the Massey University Press team.

I am grateful to artists John Pule and Gregory O'Brien for allowing one of their fine collaborative etchings to grace the cover of this book. This etching hangs on the wall of my study and captures precisely my feeling for the sea. Diving into its depths is an invitation, a revelation and an adventure.

It was my father who instilled in me a love of the sea. One of my earliest memories is of him carrying a red-painted dinghy down a muddy track to the sea from the family bach at Whangaparāoa. He carried it on his back, turtle fashion, and that is how I have carried dinghies ever since I was strong enough to lift them. A memory from teenage years is of getting up before dawn during summer holidays at Russell, hoping with youthful fervour that the weather would be suitable for fishing. Dad would be standing outside in the waning darkness, studying the clouds overhead to discern the wind strength. If the clouds were scudding too fast there would be no boating for us that day. But on days when the clouds were sluggish we would launch his runabout and head out to the Bay of Islands in search of snapper, kahawai and gurnard. I am a saltwater person because of him, and I hope always to be one. As Keri Hulme wrote, 'the sea has all our dreams'.

Introduction

The sounding of the whale

I N THE OPENING SCENE of Jacques Cousteau's first feature film, *The Silent World*, seven divers, each holding aloft a torch of blazing phosphorus, descend into the deep. The camera follows them down, tracking through the bubbles of hot gas that swell and rise like white mushroom caps to the surface. On the seafloor, 50 metres down, the divers fan out to explore and film a coral reef. Over the Darth Vader rasp of their breathing comes the voice of the narrator: 'These divers, wearing the compressed-air aqualung, are true spacemen, swimming free as fish.'

Cousteau released *The Silent World* in 1956, the year I was born. Over the next four decades, his movies and television documentaries would make him a household name, his adenoidal French accent as familiar in his day as David Attenborough's breathless British whisper is in ours.

Cousteau was 26 when he first pulled on a pair of goggles and dived into the Mediterranean. Of that experience he wrote: 'Sometimes we are lucky enough to know that our lives have been changed, to discard the old, embrace the new, and run headlong down an immutable course. It happened to me on that summer's day, when my eyes were opened on the sea.'

Cousteau's motto was 'Il faut aller voir', 'One must go and see'. Where he went and what he saw inspired millions to follow, and I was one. My own early glimpses of the undersea world were as a teenager at Tawharanui, a curving finger of land that juts into the Hauraki Gulf north of Kawau Island. On a lungful of air I became an explorer in a forest of kelp with sea urchins grazing at their bases and mullet gliding between their trunks. Under the canopy of fronds the light was dim and golden. The sense of mystery and adventure was palpable. Until I had to come up for another breath.

But then came scuba — the euphonious acronym for 'self-contained underwater breathing apparatus' — and with it the freedom Cousteau described after his first dive with an aqualung, in 1943: 'From this day forward we would swim across miles of country no man had known, free and level, with our flesh feeling what the fish scales know.'

Flying without wings, Cousteau called it. And such flights! Scuba has opened worlds beyond imagination. I have dived with harp seals in the frozen Gulf of St Lawrence, surfacing into a sea-ice slush that stung my face like needles. I hand-fed grey nurse sharks off the coast of South Africa, and once, far offshore in the Indian Ocean, where the swells reared up like mountain ranges and dolphins surfed down their faces, I leaped into the limitless blue to witness sperm whales passing.

In Belize I bobbed among a kaleidoscope of creatures encrusting the roots of mangrove trees that dangled and danced in the tide. In the Sulu Sea, in the Philippines, I turned a slow enraptured somersault as an oceanic manta ray glided above me, and in the Okavango Delta I floated with baby crocodiles in a garden of water lilies and freshwater algae.

In New Zealand's Poor Knights, an undersea canyonland of

caverns and arches that Cousteau himself visited and declared to be one of the best dive sites in the world, I once surfaced in an underwater cave and took my scuba regulator out of my mouth to breathe fresh air 10 metres under the sea. In Fiordland I explored an emerald-tinted world of strawberry sea squirts, black coral trees and pink sea pens, the ocean's living quills.

It seems remarkable that human beings started exploring space at the same time that they began diving beneath the seas of our own planet. (Sputnik was launched the year after Cousteau made *The Silent World*.) The two realms are often compared, and correctly so. In both environments a person is weightless and needs a portable air supply. And though the undersea world is far from silent, it is often a place of profound and soothing quietude.

But it is the otherness, the alienness, the sense of venturing into the unknown that is the most telling comparison. I know no other activity in which one so completely steps through the wardrobe of the familiar into a Narnia of strange sights and even stranger creatures. One moment you are an earthling, tethered to the terrestrial; the next you are, as Cousteau put it, an archangel.

It can indeed be heavenly down under. Some might even go so far as to exclaim, like Narnia's unicorn: 'This is my real country! I belong here. This is the land I have been looking for all my life, though I never knew it till now.'

As with the exploration of outer space, humans have tried to extend their visitations to the deep. Cousteau sent his 'oceanauts' to live in experimental stations on the seafloor, once for three weeks at 100 metres. (Their biggest problem at that depth was that their champagne went flat.) But short of growing gills, our sojourns in the undersea country will always be that; temporary. The important thing, as Cousteau and his torch-bearing spacemen showed, is to go and see for oneself. To go and see and have one's eyes opened.

This has been my experience, first as a child tasting adventure, later as a student studying for a degree in marine zoology, and then as a writer for *New Zealand Geographic* and *National Geographic*. I like to think I have been taking soundings — a traditional nautical term for the act of determining the depth of water, but also a phrase that has come to mean testing ideas and seeking knowledge.

Whales also sound, when they forsake the surface for the deep. I find it a beguiling thought that our big-brained kin, possessing a social intelligence we can scarcely begin to imagine, are sounding their world and probing its depths.

On my desk as I write these words lies a curiously shaped piece of bone, ivory-coloured and pitted all over its surface. It is about the size of a large potato and fits comfortably into my hand, so that my fingers can curl partly around it. The underside is flattened and split by an opening into its hollow interior. It belonged to my Canadian great-uncle, who in old age came to live with his daughter and her family in Auckland. He was a shell collector. I was a young boy who had started to collect shells, and he gave me several ornate specimens to enlarge my collection. He also gave me this: the eardrum of a sperm whale.

If I hold the opening to my ear, as one would do with a triton shell or a conch, I can hear the sea. I am holding it now, typing with one hand. I am listening with my human ear, through the ear of one of the most legendary of sea creatures, to the sound of the ocean, from which all life came.

Were I to trace the whakapapa of this eardrum back far enough in time, I would find something startling: the ancestors of whales lived on land. For millions of years, they were land mammals, like us. Then they returned to the sea. In a way, divers follow them back.

Cousteau said he often felt a trespasser in the sea. It seems an odd word for him to use. Trespass suggests transgression, entry without permission. I do not feel like a trespasser when I descend into the sea. Perhaps a foreigner, someone who has come to another country and is still learning its language and its ways. It may take a lifetime to learn, and then only imperfectly. Increasingly, however, that country begins to feels like home.

A life
aquatic

I UNLOCK THE CHAIN THAT tethers the dinghy to a pōhutukawa root on the Russell esplanade and pull the little boat down over the smooth, rattling pebbles of the beach towards the water. I have known this beach for more than half a century. I skimmed its chocolate-coloured pebbles across the water when I was a child and have watched my own grandchildren do the same. I used to 'bake' my children in an umu made by heaping these sun-warmed stones on their bodies until only their mouths and nostrils showed. They would lie still until the heat or the claustrophobia got to them, then rise up like Lazarus, stones falling from their limbs, and dive into the sea.

It is autumn now, and my father is with me. We carry a chilly bin and food box, bedding, overnight bags, tools and paraphernalia down the steep beach to the dinghy. I take the oars and Dad pushes us off, manoeuvring his weak leg slowly over the transom and in. He had a hip replacement a few years ago. I'm in line for the same surgery. Like father, like son. I hope I do as well as he does at 92.

I row out to a white-hulled launch moored 50 metres off the beach, lift one of the oars from its rowlock and steady the dinghy against the stern. Dad steps onto the duckboard — not an original feature of the boat but one that makes life easier for everyone — and unzips the awning.

There are rituals in all facets of boating, and the moment of entry is one. I fish for the keys in a pot of clothes pegs and unlock the varnished kauri doors that open to the saloon. The interior is cool and dim. There are only eight small portholes and two sets of skylights to allow light to enter — not like modern launches with their capacious windows. But we appreciate the den-like feeling of enclosure. It's how boats were designed in the era when *Marline* was built.

We stow our stores and belongings, switch on the batteries and start the engine. I walk up on deck to cast off the mooring rope, and give a mental farewell to Russell's waterfront: the Duke of Marlborough hotel, the Four Square grocery store, the swordfish club, a clutch of houses and restaurants, historic Pompallier House, a long row of pōhutukawa overtowered by a single massive Moreton Bay fig tree. All this I have known from childhood, and most of it my father has known from his childhood. He was born here.

His father, Leon, had come to the Bay of Islands after returning from World War I. He met my grandmother, Phyllis, in Whangārei Hospital, where she nursed him as he recovered from shrapnel injuries. Leon had trained as a boatbuilder in St Marys Bay in central Auckland before the war. In the 1920s he and his brother George, a marine engineer, established a boatbuilding business at Matauwhi Bay, at the entrance to Russell, and lived in adjacent houses a few hundred metres up the road. Their boatshed is still standing, now converted into clubrooms for the Russell Boating Club. George's bungalow is also standing, owned by my father and mother as a holiday home. Leon's house burned down some time after he had retired and moved back to St Marys Bay in 1941.

When Leon and George arrived in the bay, big-game fishing in New Zealand was in its infancy. That would change rapidly when Zane Grey, an American sportfisherman and writer of pulp westerns, came to New Zealand in 1926 to catch marlin, mako sharks, yellowtail kingfish and whatever else he could hook as he trolled in the Bay of Islands and along the Northland coast from the Poor Knights to Whangaroa. The book he published about his fishing exploits (including trout fishing around Taupō) helped establish New Zealand as 'the angler's El Dorado'.

Grey hired two local skippers to take him and his buddy Captain Laurie Mitchell fishing. Grey fished from Francis Arlidge's launch, *Alma G*; Mitchell fished with my grandfather from his launch, *Marlin*. Almost a hundred years later, Dad and I are following in their wake.

We idle past the historic Russell wharf, with its crane for weighing the big fish that come in on the game-fishing boats. When I was a boy, it was a summer ritual to walk to the wharf in the late afternoon, count the triangular flags fluttering from the flagpole, showing which fish had been caught that day, and then watch them being winched up from the transoms of the fishing launches and weighed. Weigh-ins are rare today. Most of the striped marlin hooked by anglers are tagged and released. A fish is kept if the angler thinks it may be a record, or if it is early in the season, when freezers are empty and palates are craving the taste of smoked marlin.

More than ninety per cent of the game fish caught in New Zealand are striped marlin. For some reason, perhaps because we're on the edge of the striper's geographical range, we get the big fish — the ones that have the muscle to travel farthest. Sixteen of the 22 line-class world records for striped marlin are for fish caught in New Zealand waters, including the all-tackle world record of 224 kilograms, caught off the Tūtūkākā coast in 1986.

The other species of marlin that was common in my grandfather's day, but is almost never encountered today, is the black marlin. Black marlins were monsters. They were the big prize for an angler, or swordfishermen as they were called back then. Swordfishing, however, is a misnomer. The true swordfish, effusively described as the 'gladiator of the deep', 'the animated torpedo of the Seven Seas' and 'the greatest fighting fish in the world', is eagerly sought but rarely caught by New Zealand anglers. The swordfish earns its name from the fact that its bill, which can reach up to half the length of its body, is flattened like a broadsword, whereas marlin bills are round, like a spear. Very few swordfish (or broadbills, as they are usually referred to today) were caught here until the late 1980s, when specialised techniques such as drift fishing at night with chemical lightsticks were used to target them.

The publication of Grey's book led to an influx of anglers to the Bay of Islands. Leon and George found they could make a living building boats in the winter and taking clients big-game fishing in the summer, a seasonal division of labour that has always struck me as an enviable combination. Their names feature regularly on the catch boards that have pride of place in the Russell swordfish club: varnished kauri panels engraved with the names of anglers, boats, skippers and the weight of the fish they landed.

In the early years of big-game fishing, catches were quoted in cumulative poundage, as if fish were timber trees to be measured in board feet. One Bay of Islands angler, an Englishman by the name of White-Wickham, reported catching 3087 pounds in 19 days' fishing in 1922 and 4924 pounds over 30 days in 1926/27. Such catches are unrepeatable today. The big fish simply aren't there.

D ad gives *Marline* some throttle and her bow lifts a few centimetres, the equivalent, I suppose, of raising her chin. Like many launches of *Marline*'s vintage, she has a displacement hull, heavy and rounded, and this design governs her speed. We cruise at a stately 7 knots.

Marline was Leon's last launch. Kauri from cabin top to keelson, she was built in 1949 in Leon's boatshed in St Marys Bay, just a few dozen metres from his house. Dad remembers helping out in the shed. One of his jobs was to hold the dolly, a piece of lead that was used to provide resistance when driving copper nails through the hull planks into the ribs. The holder was inside the boat while the hammerer was outside. It required concentration to hold the dolly at precisely the spot where the rivet was being driven, so that it would penetrate cleanly. Dad remembers his father calling out, 'You're not on it! You're not on it!'

Leon sold *Marline* a few years after he built her. The foreshore in front of his property was being reclaimed in preparation for building the Auckland Harbour Bridge and Westhaven marina. No longer able to row out to his boat on her mooring, he decided not to keep her.

Marline was out of the family for 30 years, much of it in Tauranga, where she was used in big-game fishing around Tūhua Mayor Island. It was a sheer fluke that my father, driving across Panmure bridge in east Auckland, happened to glance down at the boats moored in the Tāmaki River and thought that one of them looked familiar. It was *Marline*, somewhat altered but still recognisable, and in 1986 he was able to buy her back. It was a happy day when we motored into Russell for the first time, restoring a nautical connection: a Warne boat in the bay once more.

Now we are taking *Marline* back to Auckland, her winter home. We pass familiar landmarks as we leave the bay: the white flagpole at Waitangi across the water; the inlet that runs up to Kerikeri; the Black Rocks, one of which has the shape of a battleship; and the Ninepin, a triangular fin of rock that was a reliable spot for catching kahawai, which congregate around such pinnacles.

As we approach Tāpeka Point, the tip of the Russell Peninsula, we feel the lift of the ocean swell — always a thrilling first taste of the voyage to come. We round the point and take the inside route, between the islands and mainland, towards Cape Brett. In calm weather we sometimes take the more direct outside route, past Red Head, the tip of the outermost island, but the inside passage is so full of memories, of fishing and picnicking and overnighting in secluded bays, that we prefer it. I think of the many times I paddled my kayak here from Russell, beached it on a sandbar and snorkelled for scallops.

At Urupukapuka, the largest of the islands, we anchor in historic Otehei Bay, and it feels like a homecoming. This was the bay where Grey, Mitchell, Arlidge, my grandfather and their boatmen based themselves for the three months of Grey's fishing trip. Grey chose Otehei Bay because he wanted a camp all to himself. He could have gone to Deep Water Cove, an established anglers' base a few kilometres towards Cape Brett, but that would have meant fraternising with other anglers, and that was not his style. He liked to run his 'outfit', as he called it, in his own way. So he leased a few acres and set up camp.

It was to be my grandfather's first and last fishing season with Grey. In an interview for the *New Zealand Weekly News* in 1971 he said, 'I was with him one year and then I fell out with him. Unfortunately I don't know quite how it happened. He had written an article for the *New Zealand Herald* and something in it was not quite right. I told him so and after this I was not too popular.'

That 'something' was probably Grey's claim that the locals were Philistines when it came to angling technique. He dismissed his hosts as 'mere novices at the game . . . with no realisation whatever of this grandest of sport'. Wrote Grey: 'The New Zealand angler, when he got a bite, merely held his rod up and let the boatman run the boat in the direction the fish wanted to go. He did not strike the fish hard, as we do. He did not bend the rod, or pump the fish hard as we do. He followed the fish out to sea, and several hours later returned with or without the fish, mostly without.'

It must have cut the egotistical Grey to the bone that during that fishing season it was his sidekick, Captain Mitchell (an assumed title — Mitchell was neither a military nor a boating captain), who caught a world-record 976-pound (443 kilogram) black marlin from Leon's launch.

'I don't think I'll ever recover from the sight of that fish and my miserable misfortune,' Grey wrote to his long-suffering wife, Dolly. Miserable misfortune? Grey had been hauling in marlins and mako sharks hand over fist. Two days before Mitchell's triumph, Grey had landed the first broadbill to be caught on rod and reel in New Zealand waters.

Yet in *Tales of the Angler's Eldorado* he lays on his misery with a trowel. 'What a fish!' he writes. 'I, who had loved fish from earliest boyhood, hung round that Marlin absorbed, obsessed, entranced and sick with the deferred possibility of catching one like it for myself. How silly such hope! Could I ever expect such marvellous good luck? . . . Oh the madness of a fisherman! The strange something that is born, not made!'

Mitchell's fish was indeed a monster. A hand-coloured photograph shows the fish hanging by its tail from a tripod of wooden poles on the beach at Otehei Bay. Mitchell stands next to it, wearing his trademark cheesecutter cap, buttoned-up shirt and waistcoat, every inch the British sportsman Grey makes him out to be (though he was actually Canadian). The pectoral fin is at chest height, while the tip of the bill is almost touching the sand. The fish was close to 4 metres long, and the bill was 'as thick as a spade handle at the point', wrote Grey.

The *New Zealand Herald* conjectured that had the marlin been weighed when caught it would likely have passed the 1000-pound (453-kilogram) mark. Mitchell had landed the fish 10 miles off the Cavalli Islands, which lie between the Bay of Islands and Whangaroa Harbour, and did not get back to the Urupukapuka camp until evening. The fish, hoisted on the tripod and left there overnight, disgorged seven snapper. Even thus lightened, it was unweighable: the scales at Russell had a 600-pound limit. The fish had to be cut into three pieces. Noted the *Herald*: 'It was no easy job but a butcher with a saw finally settled it under the superintendence of the fishing club secretary, with a well-known Auckland medical man giving occasional advice from the standpoint of the surgeon.'

I row ashore and walk to the spot where, near as I can figure it, the tripod stood. Pop music blares from the restaurant of the current incarnation of the Zane Grey Sporting Club, renamed the Otehei Bay Resort. Most of the original buildings burned to the ground in 1972, but the same layout of cabins and a central dining room has been retained in the new lodge.

I watch a stingray glide under the wharf, a black diamond on the pale sand. For several years a semi-submersible vessel operated here as a tourism venture, offering visitors the chance to eyeball snapper and reef fish without having to don a mask and flippers. That venture ended and was replaced by dolphin-watching catamarans of ever-increasing size. Now dolphins are a rare sight in the bay, perhaps driven off by all the attention they were receiving, and dolphin watching is no longer a tourism offering.

Their absence, like that of the billfish, feels personal. So often when we were motoring in the bay a pod of bottlenose dolphins would ride *Marline*'s bow wave to the delight of everyone on board. There would be a rush to the bow to watch them twist and turn, peel off and then swim back, rolling on to their sides to watch the humans watching them.

New regulations now limit boat speed to five knots in certain parts of the bay, and prohibit approaching or swimming with dolphins, in the hope that they will return. Humans, it seems, must always be in the position of rectifying damage rather than preventing or avoiding it.

We leave Urupukapuka and weave between the rocks of the Albert Channel, past Hope Reef and into deeper water that is inky black, rather than blue-green. The water looks 'fishy', my father says. I let out trolling lines and we make a few circuits around Mahenotapuku Bird Rock, a guano-frosted slab where gannets occupy the upper storeys and gulls the ground-floor roosts. In Leon's day, the stretch between here and Cape Brett was 'marlin alley'. I can't begin to calculate how many lines and trolled baits have cut these waters, how many sharks and billfish were taken.

I find it hard to imagine Grey, Mitchell and others like them wanting to catch those magnificent fish every day for months on end. It was a kind of craving, an addiction. Grey considered himself incurable, a martyr to rod and reel.

We pick up a couple of kahawai on lures and head for Cape Brett. Soon the lighthouse comes into view, a dazzling white tower on a steep grassy slope. The light has shone here for over 100 years, initially kerosene-powered, now solar. An early keeper, Robert Wilson, used his time off to go after game fish from a 12-foot rowboat. On one occasion he hooked a mako and was towed half a mile out to sea. After bringing the animal to the side of the boat he gripped the trace with his hand to keep the shark's mouth hard up against the gunwale while the tail thrashed the sea to a froth. Wilson's gloveless hand dripped blood from cuts made by the wire leader.

In a hook of sheltered water back from the cape, Dad brings *Marline* close to the cliffs and reminisces about the day in 1951 when he was at this same spot, in the same boat, with Leon. They'd had a hard, luckless morning trolling in rough seas, and came in here for respite from the weather while they had a bite of lunch. The lines were left out on the outriggers, the kahawai baits dangling straight down in the water. Father and son were in the saloon, having a cuppa.

'One of the reels went *tick, tick, tick*, and the line came off the outrigger peg,' Dad recalls. 'The old man went out to have a look. He felt the line for a minute, and said, "Probably snapper nibbling the bait." A few minutes later it happened again. *Tick, tick, tick.* Then the reel screamed, and I jumped up and went for the rod, belting my head on the door frame and nearly knocking myself out.' The nibbling snapper turned out to be a striped marlin — a pinfish, no less, the heaviest caught in the season. My father still rubs his forehead tenderly at the memory of the splitting headache he had while he fought that fish.

We head towards the cape, a passage we always approach with respect for the combinations of wind and tide that make it unpredictable. We've been here on windless days when oily swells sucked at the weed on the Cape Brett rocks and the tidal race eddied the dark water. And we've felt the teeth of northeast gales, when *Marline*'s round-bilged hull rolled drunkenly through alarming arcs, tipping charts and rods off their shelves in the saloon. Today we have calm seas and an entourage of dolphins and pseudorca, a species related to pilot whales, leading us through the gap between the cape and Motukōkako Piercy Island with its famous 'hole in the rock'.

The cliffs of the cape are scarred battlements that have endured the battering ram of the sea. I've seen these blackened ramparts covered with what looked like snowflakes but showed through binoculars to be a rabble of roosting gulls, made miniature by the scale of the rock. Grizzled pōhutukawa cling to the clifftops, many stripped to staghorn skeletons by possum browsing, but others flushed with fresh growth thanks to a pest eradication programme. Boatmen in Leon's day used to shoot goats off the cliffs from their launches and pick up the carcasses from the sea.

We see a few game-fishing boats creeping along the horizon at the 200-metre contour where the water changes colour from black to deep blue. Anglers call it the blue line. Dad and I hooked a marlin out here once, so long ago I can barely remember the details. We were trolling lures and a fish struck and tore off a couple of hundred metres of line. We were so shocked it took a few moments to realise what was happening. At the end of its run the fish leaped once. It was a marlin. Then the line went slack. When I reeled it in I found the heavy nylon leader had been rasped through. The fish must have got its bill around it. One glimpse was all I had, but that image of a marlin rampant, a sun-drenched thing of wild beauty, has never left me.

Past the cape we turn south, heading for an overnight anchorage near Whangamumu Harbour. We pass Waiwiri Rock, where white-fronted terns flutter up and settle back down each time a swell breaks against the rock and sends a wash of whitewater across it. There are always trevally schooling in patches near this rock. Trevally don't take a lure, but we sometimes troll around the patches anyway, in the hope that kahawai might be lurking below.

This stretch of coast is special to me. When I was in my early teens I was invited on an Easter fishing trip, an annual gathering of the old men of the sea: Leon and his brother George, their skipper mate and Bay of Islands identity Jim Whitelaw, my father and his brother Richard, and a boy from the next generation. Previously my older brother, Geoffrey, had been chosen. This year it was my turn.

The trip had the feeling of an initiation, and I've never forgotten it. In the bay, we fished on 'George's Mudbank' and 'Jim's Sandbank', favourite fishing grounds that we located by triangulating landmarks such as a certain tree on a certain hill, a house, or the moment when a distant island came into view past a headland. There was no such thing as a chart plotter back then.

At high tide we motored quietly into a bay on Urupukapuka that was known for its lush meadows of seagrass, or eelgrass as the locals call it. Seagrass meadows are nurseries for many fish species, including piper, a long, slender fish with an elongated lower jaw that looks like a bill. Blue-green on their dorsal surface, silver-white below, they grow to about 20 centimetres in length and were popular in those days as bait and as an eating fish.

We rowed ashore with a net and threw pebbles into the water to see if there were any piper around. Each stone throw caused a dozen silvery bodies to leap out of water, so we set to, paying out the net from the dinghy then pulling it ashore using long ropes that were flicked constantly to scare the fish into the middle of the net. We caught dozens, packing the fish into wooden boxes before motoring around the cape.

At dusk the two launches anchored hard up against cliffs north of Whangamumu that drop vertically into the sea. Piper was cut up into chunks for bait, and handlines made ready. The old men preferred lines to rods for catching snapper. Rods were for sport, lines for business. This was business. I was told that the fishing would be fast and furious. There would be no time to wind the line on to its spool. I was to coil it at my feet when I rebaited or caught something, and on no account to let a fish drop onto the coiled line — that would instantly result in a bird's nest of tangled nylon and would end my fishing for the evening.

Sure enough, the fishing was spectacular. I have never experienced anything like it. As soon as the bait dropped out of sight it would be hit by a hungry fish. Then, as warned, disaster struck. A flapping snapper slipped out of my fingers and fell on the coiled line. In the darkening dusk there was no way to see clearly to untangle the line, and my fishing was over.

I watched the others until the fish stopped biting and we motored in to Whangamumu Harbour, site of a former whaling station. Jim had been a whaler there. He told stories of rowing a whaleboat from Whangamumu to Russell to buy stores — a round trip of close to 80 kilometres. It was all in a day's work, and probably a welcome respite from the monotony of scanning the sea for spouts. Jim said the snapper the whalers caught in the harbour were inedible because they had gorged on oily whale blubber. None of the whalers was ever sick, he claimed, because microbes couldn't survive the stench of rotting whale carcasses.

I watched the men fillet the snapper, admiring their dexterity. Jim could take off a fillet with a single swipe of his knife. I helped prepare the piper. They were topped and tailed, then slit along the belly. An empty tomato sauce bottle was used like a rolling pin to flatten the body. The backbone could then be lifted out and the fish sliced into rounds, ready to be mixed with batter and fried.

Piper fritters — even now my mouth waters at the thought. I still find piper sometimes in bays where we anchor. They come to the light of the boat, and if I am quick enough with a hand net I scoop a few. I would never use them for bait now. They are a rare, delicious, memorious morsel.

As the sun goes down, Dad and I set a longline from the dinghy. 'The evening rise,' I like to call it, remembering that Easter when I was a boy, though there is no rising involved with a longline. The line lies on the seabed, but snapper seem hungrier at dawn and dusk, so this is when we fish for them.

We pay out the thick nylon groundline, clipping on traces baited with kahawai. We like setting and retrieving from the dinghy, where we are close to the water. It seems simple and timeless: oars, line, hooks, bait, fish.

Dad and I built this dinghy 20 years ago in my workshop. I named her *Marlina*, to go with *Marline*. The first time we built a boat together was much earlier, when I was a teenager: a one-person Starling-class yacht. One size up from the classic P-class, the Starling was designed by one of the country's renowned yacht designers, Des Townson. Fifty years later, one of my own sons bought a Townson 32-foot yacht, and I worked with him to restore her, just as for the past 30 years I have worked with my father to restore and maintain *Marline*.

My Starling was number 284, and I named her *Mazurka*. Giving boats musical names runs in the family, arising from my mother's love of classical music and my upbringing as a pianist and violinist. She named my father's 17-foot runabout *Nabucco* after the opera, which contains one of her favourite pieces of music, 'Chorus of the Hebrew Slaves'. I'm not sure why I chose 'mazurka' — perhaps for its exotic sound and connotations of speed. Alas, speed in the name did not translate into speed on the water. We had built a sturdy boat, not a speedy boat, and I don't recall that I ever won a race.

But racing was never a priority. It was the joy and adventure of lone sailing. A boy, a boat and a breeze. Once you have felt the way wind fills a sail — one moment a flapping piece of sailcloth, the next a taut birdswing curve — and the acceleration of hull across water, you never forget. With one hand on the tiller, the other holding the mainsheet, your body is the physical link between wind and movement. I sometimes wish my grandfather had built yachts as well as launches.

I used to race the Starling off French Bay, on the Manukau Harbour. One race-day morning there was barely a puff of wind but we set off anyway, sculling our rudders to try to get some movement. Then the wind died away completely and it was glassy calm. I noticed the skippers ahead of me suddenly dive into the water. I couldn't understand what they were doing — abandoning the race and allowing me to win by default? Then a swarm of flying ants hit me, a legion of biting mandibles that produced instant, electrifying pain, and over the side I went too, into the balm of the sea.

Dad and I let the longline 'soak' for an hour, as fishermen speak of the time the gear is in the water, then pull it in and unclip several fine snapper — 'Whangamumu specials', we call them. Most have a deep pink colour, bordering on red, more intensely pigmented than snapper caught in the bay. In the last light of dusk I row us back to the boat. On board, I fillet the snapper carefully, trying to lift every skerrick of flesh from the bones. I'm nowhere near as adept as the old men on the Easter trip, but I like the feeling of being an inheritor and perpetuator of this tradition.

It's dark by the time I cook dinner, flouring a fillet each, dipping in egg and breadcrumbs and frying on the galley's little gas stove. The boat lifts and falls gently on the easterly swell that is an almost constant feature of this coast. After coffee and, for Dad, a line-up of tablets for blood pressure and heart, I will row a second anchor out from the stern to align *Marline* at right angles to the swell. Without the stern anchor, even a hint of swell will push her parallel to the waves and she will rock like a pendulum.

We wake early, breakfast simply and motor out to sea. Dew on the decks, diesel purring a sweet baritone note, white prow cleaving a blue-black sea, these are the mornings I live for. We pass harbours and bays where we have stopped for lunch or a dive over these 30 years, and remember stretches of water where we have seen special creatures: a dolphin carrying her dead calf on her nose, a whale, a sunfish.

On most passages we break the trip at Whangārei Heads, but this time we press on across Bream Bay, a crossing that always seems to pass slowly. The prevailing winds on this coast are southwest and northeast. Both strike a vessel on its beam as it crosses the bay, so there is an inevitable roll that becomes a challenge to the stomach's equanimity. We take turns steering, sleeping and reading.

Beyond the southern end of Bream Bay we pass Te Hāwere-a-Maki Goat Island, site of Leigh Marine Laboratory, Auckland University's marine research base, and of the country's first marine reserve, which was created while I was studying for my master's degree in marine zoology. My thesis subject was the classification of a group of New Zealand sponges. My supervisor was Patricia Bergquist, a world expert on these animals. It was her lectures when I was an undergraduate that sparked my interest in marine invertebrates in general and sponges in particular.

I travelled around the country collecting specimens from rocky shores at low tide and from deeper habitats by diving and dredging, then brought them back to Auckland where I boiled off the flesh in acid and scrutinised the skeletal elements — slivers of silica known as spicules — using light microscopes and electron microscopes. Spicules come in an array of shapes and sizes which are often specific to a species and are therefore a useful basis for classifying them. Taxonomy is a kind of detective work, searching for clues to an identity. If there is no match to an existing species, the specimen could be a representative of a species new to science. I named one new species as part of my graduate work.

Rounding Cape Rodney, we enter what I think of as my home waters. Tongan-born philosopher, anthropologist, scholar and poet Epeli Hau'ofa wrote, 'There are no more suitable people on earth to be the custodians of the oceans than those for whom the sea is home.' His next words challenge me: 'We seem to have forgotten that we are such a people.' Hau'ofa was thinking especially of indigenous Pacific people, but his definition of those who know the sea as home is expansive and generous. 'Anyone who has lived in our region and is committed to Oceania is an Oceanian,' he writes. By that taxonomy, I am both a partaker of identity and a partner in custodial responsibility. I welcome both roles.

Some of the islands we pass are examples of custodianship in action. Tiritiri Matangi is one of the country's premier conservation islands, a sanctuary that thousands visit each year to see birds, reptiles and insects that no longer survive on the mainland. Other islands in Tīkapa Moana, the Hauraki Gulf, are on the same path to ecological recovery. Freed from introduced predators, they have become havens for the country's indigenous life.

I love to visit the Noises, a cluster of islands owned by the Neureuter family, who are not only reviving native ecosystems on land but are also seeking marine protection for the waters surrounding the islands. They exhibit the spirit of reciprocity that must become universal if a global tragedy of species extinction is to be averted. For the family, the privilege of ownership is married with the responsibility of stewardship. But they consider stewardship to be a privilege, too. By taking care of the land, they are taking care of their deepest selves.

For Dad and me, *Marline* also invites thoughts of stewardship. She is heritage and she is legacy, and in maintaining her we maintain something in ourselves.

We arrive at the mouth of the Tāmaki estuary, the waterway that is both the beginning of my father's reconnection with this boat, when he serendipitously spotted her at her mooring, and this voyage's end. We throttle back to 5 knots and follow a channel between boats that tug on their moorings as the tide streams past.

Once we tried to navigate this channel at night, using a paper chart that showed the port and starboard beacons marking the channel between mudflats that stretch across most of the estuary. I noted each upcoming beacon, red or green, on the chart and tried to pick them out of the plethora of lights that shone on shore. The problem with lights is that you can't readily tell how far away they are — nearby, marking the channel, or perhaps the red and green of a distant set of traffic lights. We took a wrong turning and came gently but firmly to rest on the mud. And there we stayed for the next two hours, unable to free *Marline*'s hull until the incoming tide lifted us off and we could find the channel again.

By day the navigation is easy, and in an hour we have arrived at the wooden piles that mark our place on the river. I hook up the mooring lines and make the boat secure. We perform the rituals of departure: switching off the batteries, closing portholes, skylights and hatches, locking the saloon doors. I row us to the jetty, watching *Marline* recede.

In my mind's eye, she never recedes. She embodies a link

to the sea forged in childhood explorations of the rock pools of Whangaparāoa, in my father's bedtime stories of Ole Man Swordfish and the Bluefish Boys, in the shells I collected and kept in shoeboxes. These experiences set my face to the sea and ignited my curiosity about what lies beneath. They propelled me towards marine study and, later, an attempt to put into words the sea's deep beckoning.

A tale of
two oceans

W E WERE 10 KILOMETRES off the east coast of South Africa, in the shipping lane, and the seas were like mountain ranges. The coal carrier *Nightwhisper* was steaming south at a fast clip, enjoying a few knots of assistance from the Agulhas Current, a river of water that sweeps southward from the equator and is one of the fastest flowing currents in the ocean. Mark Addison, a local boat captain, dive master and marine guide, had brought a filmmaker and me offshore to look for dolphins and whales. Ever the adventurer, Mark couldn't resist positioning his dive boat in the path of the ship and running ahead of it. We were planing at 20 knots and maintaining our distance from the ship.

There must have been half a kilometre between us, but it felt as if we were about to be crushed by its bulbous bow, which stretched almost 50 metres across and cleaved the sea like an axe. I have rarely felt more awed by a ship's formidable presence and implacable power than I did at that moment.

Yet no vessel is invincible out here in the Indian Ocean. Ships like *Nightwhisper* have been snapped in two and sunk on this coast, their backs broken by waves that can reach 30 metres high. In the 10-year period between 1981 and 1991, 30 ships were damaged or sunk by rogue waves off the coast of South Africa. Monster seas arise when waves generated by storm cells deep in the Southern Ocean propagate northwards against the southward-flowing current. Wherever wind opposes tide, waves grow steep — but this is wind against tide on steroids.

In 1974, Captain J. K. Mallory, a retired master mariner and professor of oceanography at the University of Cape Town, wrote an account of how abnormal waves can break a ship. 'The ship may be steaming at a reduced speed,' he explained, 'then suddenly without any warning the bow falls into a long sloping trough, probably greater than the length of the ship, so that she virtually ends up by steaming down hill with increased momentum. At the bottom of the sloping trough a very steep mountain of water probably more than 60 feet (18 m) high and almost about to break is racing towards the ship at up to 30 knots . . . Under these circumstances nothing can be done to help the ship overcome the tremendous pressures and weights which are about to be exerted on the hull. The ship's forepart has no time to lift to the onrushing mountain of water, hence it buries itself into the wave, which then becomes unstable and crashes down with a mighty force on to the deck.' The colossal strain of such pressure on the ship's structure is sufficient to bend or break the vessel.

The Atlantic Ocean, off the western coast of South Africa, is no less a threat to ships. The coastline of Namibia is known as the Skeleton Coast for the bones of ships that lie bleaching along its desert shore. Table Bay, below Cape Town's iconic Table Mountain, was known to mariners as the 'bay of storms'. Its history is a saga of cables parting, anchors dragging, vessels being pounded to smithereens, with hundreds of lives lost. Such is the severity of the Cape Town nor'wester that on more than one occasion entire fleets at anchor in the bay have been wrecked in a single night.

A few days before I arrived in Cape Town, the Atlantic claimed another casualty. *Ikan Tanda,* a 145-metre bulk carrier loaded with fertiliser from Chile, suffered an engine-room fire, lost power and was driven ashore by 10-metre waves near Scarborough Beach on the Cape Peninsula. I watched from the beach as salvors worked to pump out the oil bunkers before the battering seas could breach the hull and trigger an environmental disaster. A previous shipwreck, in 2000, had released 1300 tonnes of oil into the sea. On that occasion, 20,000 penguins had to be relocated to prevent their death from oiling.

Capetonians thronged the streets for a look, standing on roadsides with cameras and binoculars, speculating on whether the ship could be refloated. Cafés offered 'shipwreck specials', and Scarborough had the atmosphere of a fair. Surfers rode the shore break, treating the ship as a novelty, scooting past its immobile bow, where a pair of heavy chains led futilely to anchors that had failed to hold the ship at sea.

Several weeks later the ship was successfully refloated but was written off and scuttled 200 miles off the coast of Cape Town in the storm-prone seas that had wrecked her.

I was in South Africa with *National Geographic* photographer David Doubilet and his partner and fellow photographer Jennifer Hayes to report for the magazine on these stupendous seas. I had not expected such an opportunity. David's intended writing partner was Peter Benchley, the author, most famously, of *Jaws.* The pair had worked on other assignments together, but this one, Benchley decided, would be too physically demanding.

National Geographic had just published a story I had written about Fiordland. My editor, Oliver Payne, sent me a message to say the magazine was looking for someone to dive in 'very cold, very rough shark-infested waters'. 'You've found him,' I wrote back.

The assignment was all of those things, as well as an encounter with an underwater environment unparalleled in its diversity and abundance — a richness that arises from oceanographic conditions found in very few other places on earth.

South Africa lies like a blunt wedge between two powerful ocean systems: one warm, one cold. To the east, the Agulhas Current brings warmth-loving creatures such as turtles and whale sharks from the tropics. I dived with both at Sodwana Bay on the east coast, part of iSimangaliso Wetland Park, where the southernmost coral reefs in Africa are to be found.

At the same latitude on the west coast, the water temperature is a full 10 degrees cooler. To experience Sodwana's sea temperature on the Atlantic coast you would need to travel 1500 kilometres north. The cold sea conditions there are the result of the Benguela Current upwelling — a wind-driven upwelling from the depths.

I thought of the two oceans as titans, each presiding over a unique ecological realm and indulging in some oceanic arm wrestling along South Africa's broad southern coast. Oceanographers say that South Africa is the only place in the world where this kind of interaction occurs. In the transition zone, a combination of currents and countercurrents, eddies, meanders, retroflection zones and jets creates a dynamic environment for underwater life.

During the weeks I spent in South Africa, no two dives were the same. No two days were the same. Sometimes the seas were grey and wind-whipped, sometimes hazy and horizonless. Scrubbed clean by a cold front with wind off the Southern Ocean, the sea became blue-black with white crests. One windless evening the water was glassy and viscous, pink-hued in the dusk light.

Offshore in the Indian Ocean, the peaks and valleys of the swells lifted and lowered Mark's dive boat as if it were a bath toy. At the top of a crest we spotted dolphins: a pod a thousand strong. They were the species known as common dolphins. (True enough, they are the world's commonest dolphin.) I slipped into the water several hundred metres ahead of them and waited. They came in a rush, wavefuls of them leaping out of the faces of the ocean swells as if jet-propelled, sunlight gleaming on their cornmeal-coloured flanks. Most were adults, but I saw calves swimming beneath their mothers, in their slipstream.

Hearing a pod of a thousand dolphins on the move is like hearing rapids in a river, or an approaching rainstorm. Up close, you can make out the individual *pfffft* of blowholes opening, spent air being expelled and fresh breaths sucked in. Faintly, through the puffs and splashes, come the squeaks and squeals of dolphin communication. Underwater, where those sounds are heard at full volume, it is like being serenaded by a choir of dentist's drills. Unlike the larger bottlenose dolphins, common dolphins rarely pause to interact with humans. They have a focused intensity about them as they plough relentlessly through the sea. A sideways glance of the head, a slight roll to get a better view and, curiosity satisfied, they streak on ahead.

Mark saw a spout and drove in that direction, putting me in the water where he had seen the whale blow. The oceanic water was so clear I could see from a long way off that it was a female sperm whale and calf. I finned hard towards them but could not match their speed and watched the pair fade into the blue distance.

It was the first and only time I have seen a sperm whale underwater. I cannot think of these animals without a swarm of associations, from childhood Believe It Or Not! cards depicting them in mortal combat with giant squid, and Ahab's white whale, to the history of the 'whale fishery' in New Zealand waters and contemporary strandings on our shores.

Sperm whales are a society of wanderers. Nomads in three-dimensional liquid space, they may travel 35,000 kilometres a year and descend to crushing depths — 2 kilometres and more — staying submerged for up to an hour and a half. They possess the largest brain of any animal that has ever lived, and from their battering-ram heads they emit the loudest sounds ever recorded in nature. In a story for *New Zealand Geographic*, I wrote about sperm whale kin groups that may share communal knowledge of food resources and foraging strategies. There is evidence that sperm whale calves are suckled by more than one female, suggesting that, just as it takes a village to raise a child, it may take a pod to raise a calf.

The richness of their shared interactions causes the human mind to marvel. 'The thought of them roaming the bioluminescent depths of the ocean, their onrushing swiftness triggering millions of photon flashes, conjures images of space ships exploring galaxies far, far away,' I wrote. 'Their solicitous companionship — gently stroking one another with their

flippers, or nuzzling a furrowed flank with a bulbous brow —
must give even the most ardent reductionist pause.'

A person brings cultural knowledge into an encounter with
an animal like a sperm whale. It is inescapable — and who
knows that it isn't reciprocal? Recognition and response may
flow both ways across the species boundary. From the human
side, regret that our species slaughtered two-thirds of theirs,
awe for an animal one cetacean researcher described as 'a god
in our midst'. From theirs, what? A memory of maltreatment
leading to a desire to avoid? Or recognition that we see them
differently now, as fellow sentient beings?

When the whales had disappeared, I hoisted myself back
into the dive boat. My skin was tingling, and not just from the
adrenalin of the encounter. For these offshore dives in the
warm Agulhas Current I hadn't bothered with a wetsuit. When
I looked closely at my arms I saw they were peppered with
pinprick welts. I had noticed that the water was full of tiny
medusae, but had thought nothing of them. That was a mistake.
I itched from their stings for hours.

No marine phenomenon on the Indian Ocean coast
matches the Natal sardine run, an annual migration that
has been dubbed 'the greatest shoal on earth'. Yet by rights,
sardines — or pilchards as we know them in New Zealand
— shouldn't be on the KwaZulu-Natal coast at all. They are a
coldwater fish. Their strongholds are the cool, nutrient-rich
waters of South Africa's southern and western coasts, where
they occur in astronomically large numbers and where over
100,000 tonnes are harvested annually. But in winter an
oceanographic anomaly presents sardines with an opportunity

to extend their range. The prevailing southeast winter wind pushes warm surface water offshore and northwards. Cool, deep water upwells to replace it. This temperature inversion, coupled with an inshore countercurrent running in the opposite direction to the Agulhas Current, creates a narrow corridor along which sardines, anchovies and other Atlantic fish can move, feed and breed. Sardines stream around the stub of the continent, past Cape St Francis, past Port Elizabeth (now officially known by its Xhosa name, Gqeberha), past East London and as far north as Durban.

The arrival of these fish on the eastern seaboard, arising from nothing more than following their noses along a tongue of cold water, is winter's gift to marine predators. Bryde's whales, humpbacks, penguins, seals, gannets, dolphins, sharks and more converge for a midwinter feast.

The marine extravaganza is mirrored on land. Sardine fever grips the coastal communities of KwaZulu-Natal during the month of June. A telephone hotline tells people where the shoals are. Seine netters haul bulging catches from breakers that are black with fish.

On Illovo Beach, south of Durban, I watched a cross-section of the rainbow nation drawn by the sea's bounty. A Zulu boy stood by the water's edge, mesmerised by waves that were breaking fish, his fingers curled around a sardine he had picked up. Children nearby were scooping the sea with butterfly nets or burrowing into the folds of seine nets to pull out fish and stuff them into plastic bags, wrap them in jackets, gather them into skirts. An Indian woman, glamorous in lip liner and eye shadow, was hurrying up the beach with handfuls of fish wriggling in her manicured fingers. A barrel-chested Afrikaner talked to netters as they sorted their catch. A hundred rands a basket was the going rate — about ten New Zealand dollars for 20 kilos of fish. Imagine — fresh fish for 50 cents a kilogram!

In some years sardines shoaling along this northern coastline have beached themselves in unimaginable numbers. On one occasion the shoals were so dense that as the tide receded the water level in the bay was a metre higher than offshore. You could wade knee-deep through beached sardines as waves thick with fish brought more and more onshore.

My first sight of the sardine shoals was from the air, during a flight along the Wild Coast of what used to be known as the Republic of Transkei, now the Eastern Cape province. I was flying to meet David, Jennifer and other photographers at our camp at Mkambati Nature Reserve. The Wild Coast is well named. Beneath the aircraft, powerful swells pounded tessellated rock platforms, making them stream with whitewater. The offshore wind sent spray spiralling back over the wave crests, as if a giant irrigation system were operating. The waves were long, curling, perfectly shaped monsters that would have made a surfer weak-kneed with desire. Every few kilometres a rift in the sandstone cliffs revealed a jungle-clad river gorge running inland, and on the grassy veldt, stretching away into a smoky haze of cooking fires, zebra and wildebeest grazed.

The pilot's voice came through the headset: 'Dolphins at one o'clock!' He banked to take us over the pod and whooped with delight. Hundreds of dolphins were churning the sea. But I was focused on something else, a stain that darkened the ocean like an ink blot: shoaling sardines, heading north.

We spent weeks hunting these shoals with Mark, whose boating skills and ocean knowledge I admired. Mark grew up spearfishing on the KwaZulu-Natal coast. He dropped out of law school to launch a dive charter company with his father. They called the company Blue Wilderness.

Travelling out to the blue wilderness through the Wild Coast surf was never easy, never taken for granted. We launched in a sheltered embayment created by sandbars. Mark would circle the bay, watching the incoming sets, looking for a lesser swell to appear in the line-up. He called it looking for the ninth wave. When he sensed an opportunity he would accelerate across the foaming, broken water, aiming for the gap. Sometimes waves would re-form and begin to crest, and he would be forced to retreat to safe water. He would try again, circle back, try again, until we got through.

Returning to shore was just as adrenalin-filled. Mark would wait for a big swell to pass then accelerate shoreward on its back. 'Hold on!' he would shout as he drove the boat up onto the sand, prop spinning in air.

Mark had bolted a surf lifesaver's spotting platform to his inflatable, and at sea one of us would sit on it, scanning the horizon with binoculars like an old-time whaler searching for spouts or a marlin angler for a fin. Usually we saw gannets first, swirling like flecks of white ash above a fire. As we came closer, we could make out their butternut heads and black-trimmed wings as they plummeted into the sea in fusillades, sending up spurts of water like depth charges. They were our sentinels, signalling the presence of a baitball, an ephemeral pulse of sardine predation, a feeding frenzy.

We longed for baitballs. We wanted to be in the middle of these eruptions of predator intensity, to experience their visceral drama. But they were shortlived. Sometimes by the time we reached a baitball it would have dissipated or been consumed, the action spent. We would arrive to find only a few fish scales on the water and the lingering smell of sardine oil.

Bottlenose dolphins were the usual instigators of a baitball. They employ a cooperative hunting strategy to split off a portion of a sardine shoal and corral it into a tighter and tighter unit. Harried by the circling dolphins, the shoal becomes a frenzied mass. Bronze whalers, known to South Africans as copper sharks, materialise, as if from nowhere, thrashing through the shoal, flaying the water with their tails and flicking sardines high into the air. Their wild aggression contrasts with the methodical, almost mechanical, action of the dolphins, which make precise strafing runs, plucking individual sardines from the pack.

Above them, gannets wheel and plunge. Feeding gannets utter a constant manic chatter, a seeming seabird ecstasy at the abundance there for the taking. Wings folded to their sides, they enter the water with an audible *whump*. The initial plunge of these feathered javelins can take them down 10 metres. Sometimes they seize their target on the first dive and pop to the surface to swallow it. Otherwise they partially open their wings and use their elbows and webbed feet for propulsion, chasing the fleeing sardines and leaving green bubble trails in their wakes.

The press of frenzied sardines in a baitball is so great that individual fish are pushed above the water surface by the masses below. Once, while swimming in their midst, they pelted me like heavy hailstones, a flashing, glittering tumult.

On the rare occasions when a humpback whale was nearby we dreamed of being in a baitball when it was feeding, opening that cavernous mouth to capture a thousand sardines in a single uprushing gulp. We were never that lucky, but we were sometimes close enough to see the massive breadth of the back and the mountainous ridge of its vertebrae as the animal humped down for a dive. The last thing you see when a humpback dives is the pink underside of the tail, the perfect sweetheart curve of the flukes.

Baitballs were exciting and intense, but diving in the shoals when there was no predation was just as memorable. Once I stood on the seabed in the centre of a cylinder whose walls were sardines, each fish watching me through unblinking yellow-rimmed eyes. I sometimes snorkelled above the shoal, a mass of speckled grey backs, with here and there a flash of silver as fish tipped side-on, reflecting the sun. At times the shoals seemed to lose their cohesion and fish were oriented every which way. I watched a 3-metre copper shark glide above one shoal, leaving a furrow which closed up seamlessly after it passed: the semicircle curve of the snout, gill slits like knife cuts, slowly scything blade of the tail, sedate and powerful.

Not every day brought such moments. Some days in our search for sardine action we came up empty. We were restless searchers on a listless sea. Some days we couldn't go out at all. Storms hemmed us in on land. On one occasion, when we had been confined to camp by a storm, the main shoal gave us the slip, edging around a promontory known as Waterfall Bluff and streaming north, covering around 20 kilometres a day. We had to decamp and shift our base north to catch up with them.

In our sardine search we had the advantage of aerial reconnaissance. Every morning at first light Rob Allen, a South African speargun manufacturer and dedicated sardine chaser, would launch his microlight and radio the location of the shoals and any baitball activity he saw. Powered by a snowmobile engine, his machine could take off from beach or clifftop and cruise at 80 kilometres per hour, covering far more ocean than we could hope to cross by boat.

One afternoon I joined him in the passenger seat and saw manta rays carving trails through the turbid inshore water. Two sharks were following them. Seen from above, their modes of swimming made a striking contrast. Mantas flex their black wings like birds. Sharks flex their tails side to side, sinuous as crocodiles. The mantas were powering through the water, creating a wake that looked like a blue tear in the green fabric of the sea. We circled over a humpback whale that was lolling upside down, its pleated throat and long pectoral fins shining milky white.

In the evenings we cooked on a braai, grilling boerewors — long coils of spicy sausage — and occasionally a spatchcocked pullet bought from the local village. A pot of rib-sticking pap — maize meal boiled and whipped to the consistency of mashed potato — provided carbs. I developed a fondness for Afrikaans cuisine: biltong, cheap, chewy and made from all manner of bush animals — impala, eland, gemsbok, kudu; koeksister — deep-fried dough soaked in syrup, sickly sweet and delicious. I ate bobotie and potjiekos, a stew simmered in a three-legged cast-iron pot. In Cape Town I ate snoek, a metre-long type of mackerel, hot from the braai and slathered with apricot jam. In Durban I ate bunny chow: curried lamb served in a hollowed-out loaf of bread.

One evening on the Wild Coast we took the inflatable up the saline Mkambati River and found ourselves in a swarm of jellyfish. Their pale mauve bells had feathered edges and trailed a plume of thick tentacles. We bought three salmon from boys fishing in the river for 20 rands (roughly two New Zealand dollars) plus two KitKats.

Early one morning we heard Rob Allen on the radio from his microlight reporting 'four volcanoes between Grosvenor and Waterfall Bluff'. A volcano is sardine-chaser vernacular for sardine shoals pushed to the surface by sharks. But by the time we were on the water the volcanoes had gone dormant. Instead, we found fur seals lying supine on the glassy sea. They lounged on their sides with a flipper in the air to keep them cool. It looked as if they were saluting us.

Underwater, seals are masters of manoeuvrability. With their flippers outstretched they look as if they are flying. They corkscrew through a shoal, then flip on their backs and make a backwards dive into the sardines. We rarely saw them feeding — mostly they were herding the shoal, sometimes powering up through the centre, causing the fish to part around them, like a hole in a sardine doughnut.

Fur seals have a way of looking at a human diver by arching themselves upside down and studying you with their saucer eyes. Their instant acceleration leaves streams of bubbles trailing from their fur. Their whiskers reminded me of a British army colonel from the Boer War.

On one occasion we saw a pod of bottlenose dolphins herding a large shoal inshore towards the breakers to concentrate the sardines and make them easier prey. The rhythm of bottlenose dolphin travel is a steady repeating sequence: surface–blow–arch–dive. Suddenly, on some signal indiscernible to humans, they all plunge forward in double time, churning the sea white with their passage. Then they slow to the hypnotic languor of cruising mode.

In shallow water, bottlenose dolphins rotate their heads in an exaggerated way. A dolphin biologist explained to me that this helps with echolocation accuracy: the wider apart the points of transmission of the sound, the more data can be deduced from sonic reflections off underwater objects. But what a curious thing to see a group of dolphins observing you, making wide circles with their heads, as if trying to fathom the tank-toting, mask-wearing, neoprene-skinned creature in their midst.

As we approached the shoal, Mark studied his depth finder. Shoals were sometimes so dense that the depth finder would lose contact with the seabed, instead reading the top of the shoal as the bottom of the sea. I sat on the side of the inflatable, kitted up, ready to dive. 'They're under you now,' Mark said. 'Go.' So I did, and descended through that myriad host, tens of thousands of fish with their mouths open, gaping, eyes expressionless, the shoal opening as I passed through then closing again over me. Their bodies sucked up all the light. At the seabed, with all that glittering flesh tight-packed above me, it was as dark as an eclipse.

After the dive, Mark motored close to the wave-battered ramparts of the coast. He switched off the engine and let the inflatable rise and fall with the swells that broke barely 50 metres away. The offshore wind flung the tops of the waves back towards us in long bridal veils of misty spray.

I have a photograph of that scene on the wall of my study. The bare black cliffs look like something out of Tolkien, the spume-flecked seas from Conrad. The image transports me to that wild coast, which David called the Serengeti of the sea.

O ur *National Geographic* coverage of South Africa's seas needed stories of many habitats in many locations.

One place I knew I had to dive was off the Cape of Good Hope. Sir Francis Drake called it 'the fairest cape in the whole circumference of the earth', but Portuguese mariner Bartolomeu Dias, the first European to round the southern tip of Africa, dubbed it Cabo das Tormentas, the cape of storms, the destroyer of ships.

Dense fog covered the sea on the morning I set out to dive the cape. With me was Eric Simpson, one of the boat drivers and dive guides from the sardine run. We were heading for a reef called Bellows, just off the tip of the cape. Its name, and that of its neighbour, Anvil, give fair warning that a boat can be hammered out here in this smithy of the seas. Not on this day. The sea was oily smooth and the same leaden colour as the sky.

As we approached the cape, fishing boats materialised out of the fog. 'Snoek,' said Eric, and his eyes lit up. When not working as a cameraman, boat driver and commercial diver, he fishes for snoek. Eric drove over and called out a greeting to a couple of the skippers. Most of the boats were fibreglass runabouts, or ski boats, as they're called here. Fishers lined the sides of the boats, each handling two or three handlines, pulling in the long silver fish hand over hand, swinging them aboard one after the other.

Watching his fellow fishers made Eric envious. 'You can't know how this is hurting my fisherman's heart,' he said, reaching into a locker for the handline he kept there for just this sort of occasion. He flung a lure over the side and moments later he was lifting a flapping snoek over the gunwale, a big grin on his face. We couldn't stay for more, but at least we had a fish for the braai.

At the cape the cloud rolled back and the lighthouse showed. Gulls and cormorants wheeled about the cliffs. I imagined mariners of old creeping along this coast, peering into the mist, cursing the lack of wind as their ships drifted towards the cliffs where surf boomed its warning.

We slipped into the water and descended to a jumble of truck-sized rocks on the seafloor. If the sardine run is the epitome of the ocean's bounty on the KwaZulu-Natal coast, then the rock lobster is the animal that defines the richness of the cold Atlantic coast. On other dives I had seen them holed up in clefts and crevices, feelers waving defensively at the entrances, but here they were everywhere, skittering about in the open on their long, slender legs, or shooting away with a sudden snap of their tail. One adventurous crustacean had climbed a sea fan and was clinging to it like a mountaineer. Another was inside the barrel of a sponge. I swam into a thicket of the creatures for the pleasure of seeing the pell-mell scurry and scatter of a thousand lobster limbs.

Red bait — fat maroon sea squirts the size of chimney pots and thick as an old boot — were jammed together on canyon walls, often with juvenile lobsters and Cape rock crabs perched on them. If I came too close to a crab it would launch itself into the abyss, gliding down, legs outstretched. I thought of red bait as the wineskins of the sea — ancient, leathery bladders with spouts. I cradled one in my hands like a rock melon, and the water-filled cask slowly deflated, as if the life was passing from it. I passed beds of mussels with spiny starfish, orange with purple tips to their arms, dispersed across them, each one hunched over the mussel it was prising open.

I saw brick-red sea stars, bubblegum-pink coldwater corals and a four-cornered box jellyfish trailing long white filaments — possibly a relative of the sea wasp box jelly, whose stinging tentacles are capable of killing a person in minutes. I saw purple and apricot pompom anemones, black-and-cream feather stars and luxuriant soft corals that wafted back and forth in the surge like noodles. Red, yellow and grey sponges as thick as loaves of bread had gained a footing on the seafloor. A cavity in one of these rubbery blocks of tissue had become home to an octopus, which sealed itself in its den by winding a tentacle around the entrance, leaving just its eyes showing.

As I finned my way along a rock wall, engrossed with finger sponges and candelabra fans and all the paintbox glory of humble creatures, Eric tapped my arm and I looked up to see a dusky shark glide slowly by. With softly diffused light slanting on the splendid arch of its back it looked every inch a monarch.

The seas around Cape Town are forested by kelp. At Partridge Point in Castle Rocks marine reserve, on the False Bay side of Cape Peninsula, I finned through a jungle of sea bamboo, a type of kelp with trunks as thick as baseball bats, smooth as velvet and honey-coloured as varnished kauri. The plants rose 10 metres and more towards the surface.

Kelp forests have the character of forests on land, filled with the possibility of discovery. Pushing through the thickets of sea bamboo I felt like a nautical Livingstone or Stanley, with always the prospect of a new creature to see. I found rock slabs covered with grazing urchins — orange, mauve, tomato coloured, each with a prickly fuzz of fine white spines. I had read that baby abalone, known as perlemoen in Afrikaans, hide beneath urchins to evade predators. I lifted up a couple of urchins and, sure enough, three or four fingernail-sized perlemoen moved across the rock to find another shelter. Adult perlemoen need no protection, except from human harvesters. As broad as a pudding plate, with a thick fringe of sensory projections extending from beneath their massive shells, they graze the forest floor, often trapping a kelp frond under the edge of the shell so they can get better purchase for their rasping tongue.

Also grazing the algal turf were snails the size of grapefruit and giant chitons, whose chunky overlapping skeletal plates gave them the appearance of having just crawled out of the Devonian era.

Among the hottentots, red romans and other kelp forest fish I saw shysharks, their skin an elegant dapple of chocolate and fawn, and striped catsharks, also known as pyjama sharks. These small, lithe sharks curl into a ring when threatened, covering their eyes with their tails and drifting about like a cartilaginous quoit until the danger has passed. Under a ledge I saw several sleeping in a stack, one on top of another, and I found a shyshark egg case, delightfully known as a mermaid's purse, attached to a kelp frond. It was the colour and shape of a large ravioli.

One of the cleverest adaptations in this environment is that of the kelp limpet, the curvature of whose shell matches exactly that of a thick kelp trunk. Juvenile limpets live together on the fronds, but when it comes time to stake a claim to the trunk, territoriality comes into play. One mollusc per stipe is the rule, and enforcement involves a shoving contest where the winner takes all.

One of our marine guides in South Africa, Charles Maxwell, liked to paraphrase Samuel Johnson and say, 'When a man is tired of False Bay he is tired of diving.' I believe him. But it's not always possible to dive or even launch a boat here. False Bay faces due south. Antarctica, 3000 kilometres away, sends its greetings in the form of a cold, biting southeast wind, known as the Cape Doctor. At Muizenberg Beach I watched anglers in wetsuits and windbreakers cast their whippy carbon-fibre rods into the teeth of this wind as it came belting into the bay, piling up the seas into a dumping surf. The sky was often filled with the gaudy splashes of kitesurfers' parafoils. On shore, land yachts sped around a track.

On a day when, blessedly, the Doctor was off duty, I paddled to a penguin colony at Boulders, a white-sand beach on Cape Peninsula. Residents here have an unusual problem with wildlife visitors: baboons in the front yard, penguins out back. You could be forgiven for thinking you were in a donkey ranch rather than a penguin sanctuary — this species used to be known as the jackass penguin for its braying call, but has been renamed the less derogatory African penguin.

I launched from Simonstown and headed towards the colony. As I approached the beach, 20 or 30 birds clustered around my craft, shaking their heads, looking about like eager meerkats. They would swim in my direction from shore, and when they got close would dive with a splash and pop up back near shore. It took them three or four attempts before they felt confident to make a break for the open sea. False Bay is white shark territory, and no doubt the penguins have learned caution.

Glancing seaward, I spotted a triangular grey fin and my heartrate jumped. The white sharks of False Bay are famous for breaching. Seeing a fur seal at the surface, they will explode upwards, take the seal in their mouth and burst out of the water. What is a kayak but a long seal with paddle blades as fins? I paddled towards where I saw the fin, looking for the telltale shadow. What I saw brought a laugh of relief: a sunfish, deadly only to jellyfish and plankton.

A penguin flitted beneath me, flippers outstretched, a little black dart.

When I came to write the *National Geographic* story, I had more encounters to draw from than could be included in a text of a few thousand words. It surprised me that one of the experiences I treasured most, and felt must be written about, was a dive in a polluted estuary amid discarded tyres, spark plugs, beer bottles and fishing lures.

I had travelled to the town of Knysna on the Garden Route, the coast road that runs through the Western and Eastern Capes, because I had heard about a conservation ranger who had an abiding interest in the marine life of its estuary and a particular love for one of its most precious inhabitants: a diminutive seahorse found only here and in a few nearby saltwater lagoons.

When I met him, Peet Joubert described his role as a combination of water-speed cop, building inspector and pollution checker. 'The estuary,' he said, 'is my hobby, my passion, my life.' But the health of its marine environment was deteriorating from the pressures of human development. Declining water quality, algal blooms, loss of habitat and invasive species were all causing concern. Knysna's seahorse was threatened by the estuary's degraded state.

Peet offered to show me around the seahorse's domain, such as it was. But first he had a surprise. He walked across his office to an aquarium, picked up a wooden ruler and started prodding a rock. Out fluttered a seahorse, caramel-coloured with dark brown blotches. It glided to the corner of the tank where another seahorse had its tail twined around a piece of seaweed.

'They mated three weeks ago,' Peet said proudly. 'You can see the eggs in the male's pouch.'

I bent closer, and through the translucent skin of the male's belly I could make out a clutch of eggs. It wasn't hard to see how someone could develop an affection for these animals — in Peet's case nurtured over a dozen years of observing them. He has watched them court and mate, and watched them give birth. The young, which are released live from the male's pouch, are the size of mosquito larvae. 'These damned stupid things are just fish,' Peet joked, 'but there's something about them.'

We donned snorkelling gear and walked down a slipway into the water, then finned across a seagrass meadow where pale sea hares grazed. We saw cuttlefish, feather stars and baby octopus. Giant Knysna mud crabs with carapaces as wide as an outspread hand flexed their pincers as we passed.

Seagrass is seahorse habitat, too, and soon we found one. The little fellow curled its tail around my finger and laid its head against my palm. I have rarely felt as tenderly touched by a marine creature as by that hippocampus.

With scuba tanks, Peet and I dived in another part of the estuary, a seeming desert of grey silt with dead shells scattered across its surface, along with the random discards of a town of 75,000. Visibility was less than a metre. It was like diving in fog. Peet said the best way to explore was by 'finger walking'; using fins would kick up too much sediment.

I wasn't expecting to find much in this world of silt and throwaways, but the place was a revelation. In the estuary's sheltered waters, many organisms grow large and luxuriant. Sponges form fat cushions, road-paint yellow and soapy to the touch. Tubeworms in pastel shades of salmon and white make graceful sweeps of the water with their plankton-catching feather-duster crowns. At the merest touch the whole feathery canopy retracts in a flash, leaving just the dull, naked tube.

Fat, purple-speckled sea hares grazed over beds of seagrass

while their gaudier relatives, the nudibranchs or sea slugs, cruised colourful avenues of sea squirts and anemones. A starfish was hunched over an urchin: echinoderm eating echinoderm. Several false corals, a type of bryozoan, had the form of rose petals, their pore-dotted curves resembling the most delicate porcelain.

I heard an oddly melodic sound and saw that it was Peet humming to himself. Here was a man in his element, riffling his fingers through clumps of green alga to flush out shrimps, feeling under the rims of tyres for mudfish, and spelling out the names of things in the silt for my benefit. He pointed to a brick-red encrusting organism with daffodil-yellow siphons and wrote T U N I C A T E. I recognised another member of this group of sea squirts and pointed to it: transparent tubes with fine cream lines running down their sides and around their mouthlike openings. They are called choirboy tunicates on account of the cherubic 'O' of their mouths.

Peet picked up a glass jar and starting tapping it, then whacking the bottom with his hand. I wondered what he was doing. Then he held it upside down, took his scuba mouthpiece from his mouth and started filling it with air. A purple tentacle emerged from the jar, then another, and finally an entire octopus made a dash for somewhere new to hide, departing with a defensive squirt of black ink.

Back in Peet's office, warming up over a cup of tea, he told me that Knysna is the most important estuary in South Africa for biodiversity; it boasts more species even than the vast iSimangaliso wetlands. Yet keeping a brake on development is a constant battle. Peet felt that he had only to turn his back and another piece of habitat would go under the bulldozer blade.

He spoke of estuarine phenomena he had seen, such as

mass cuttlefish matings in Langebaan Lagoon on the west coast, carpets of purple sea cucumbers and Knysna mud crabs with claws as big as a human fist. 'Sorry if I yack,' he said, 'but this stuff gets me excited. I'm totally nuts about the South African coast because there's so much variety. I'm a kid in a candy store.'

I felt the same way. Over the previous weeks I had chased sardines on the Wild Coast, kayaked with penguins at Simonstown, cage-dived with white sharks at Gansbaai, hand-fed ragged-tooth sharks at Aliwal Shoal, witnessed the mass spawning of arrow squid at Cape St Francis, viewed a shipwreck and swum with humpback, right and sperm whales. I had seen sunfish, moon wrasse, white-bar rubberlips, spotted toby, clown triggerfish, semicircle angelfish, honeycomb moray, vagabond butterfish, ember parrotfish, musselcracker, Moorish idol, silverflash spinecheek, oval moony, longspine pursemouth, dusky cherub, jumping bean, chocolate dip. Just writing down their names makes a poem.

One encounter continues to astound me. I was floating face down in cold, turbid water off the south coast, a place called Franskraal. In winter, right whales congregate here to mate and calve. David, Jennifer and I had permits to be in the water with these animals. Swimming with whales in South Africa is prohibited without a permit.

The water was murky, the visibility poor. Through my dive mask I saw what seemed to be the seabed. But it couldn't be. Our inflatable boat was nearby, anchored in tens of metres of water. The shadowy terrain below me slowly materialised into a moving shape, and I realised it was not the seabed but the top of a whale's head, a head that was rising steadily towards me. I saw clumps of barnacles and jagged projections of skin, part of the animal's callosity, a miniature ecosystem of organisms that right whales carry on their heads. Whalers used to refer to them as the whale's bonnet or crown. No two are the same. They are unique to each individual and offer a convenient way for biologists to identify animals from a distance.

'Callosity' sounds not dissimilar to 'colossal', which was my prevailing impression at that moment. The leviathan was surfacing, and I was in the way. For a moment, I wondered if I was about to be sliced by knife-edged barnacle shells. The species of barnacle that lives on whales (and almost exclusively on whales) can reach as long as a matchbox. Then I saw the massive tail coming towards me, like the wing of an aircraft, but thick, black and rubbery.

I finned backwards to give the animal some sea room. The whale rolled over, twisted its massive bulk and rose out of the sea inches away from me. As it rose, I reached my hands out against the animal's pure-white throat. I had the sense of pressing my fingers against a missile rising out of a bunker. Up and up it rose, a living wall of flesh, then crashed backwards, away from me, into the sea. It sank down and was gone.

I swam to the inflatable. Jennifer was on board. 'Kill me now!' I exclaimed. I felt like an Old Testament sojourner who had caught a glimpse of the Almighty. I wouldn't have been surprised if a voice said, 'Take off your fins, for the water you are treading is holy.'

I have had the same feeling in other parts of the underwater cosmos, where so much is unexpected, mysterious and profound. Profound — profond — is the word the French use for deep. As in English, it is both a measure of water and a quality of thought. Perhaps our minds and the sea are twins. Deep calls to deep.

Beneath
Arabian seas

WHEN I THINK OF Arabia I think not of oil or the desert but of the sea. I think of an old man sitting on a scrap of carpet in a thatched shelter on the coast of the Musandam Peninsula in Oman. He was toothless and had a face like a walnut shell and his eyes had the squint of a lifetime of gazing into the white-hot glare of Arabia. The summer wind, the shamal, was blowing off the sea in scorching gusts, making even the date palms droop.

'It is the western wind,' the old man croaked in his rasping voice, 'I feel its warmth.' This was an understatement. At that moment, the village of Film, notched into the arid mountains, shimmered like a brazier. Goats panted in scraps of shade cast by upturned boats and the walls of a mosque. Just breathing made me feel as if my nostrils might burst into flame. Sami Alhaj, my Yemeni dive partner, remarked: 'Underwater, with the corals, we get a little piece of heaven. Above water, with this wind, we get a little piece of hell.'

We soon fled the inferno and descended into paradise. Colour marked our passage between worlds as vividly as temperature did. Where the colours of land were those of the spice souq — pepper, cinnamon, mustard, mace — the undersea world was drenched in the sumptuous hues of a sultan's palace. Long, waving indigo arms of soft corals mingled with pomegranate fronds of feather stars. Speckled-grey moray eels, whose gaping mouths revealed a startling burst of custard yellow, leered out of crevices, while butterflyfish flitted past in tangerine flashes. Crevices bristled with black urchins; I swam too close to one and paid for my carelessness with an ankleful of spines as sharp as acupuncture needles.

Musandam juts like a fang into the Persian Gulf, poised to stab the flank of Iran. The ancient name for this part of Arabia means the anvil's head, and in the heat of midday it felt like being in a blast furnace. The peninsula is a labyrinth of waterways, like a desert version of the Marlborough Sounds. It lies at the tip of land that is mostly part of the United Arab Emirates. It is not contiguous with the rest of Oman, which lies south and east. The stretch of water separating Musandam from Iran, the Strait of Hormuz, is a channel as strategic in the past as the Suez Canal is today. Through these waters East met West, the wealth of Africa and India flowing to the empires of Britain and Europe. Oman, an empire in its own right, was the gatekeeper.

At its narrowest point the strait is a mere 50 kilometres wide. I watched Iranian smugglers bringing drugs and cheap fuel to Oman and the free-trade zones of UAE, and returning to Iran loaded with beer and spirits. Their small fibreglass skiffs sped past in groups of up to a dozen. My boat skipper said they travel in convoys so that if a patrol boat targets one, the rest get away. Pirates with much larger, faster boats regularly run down the smugglers, smashing their craft, taking the contraband and leaving the crew to swim for shore or drown.

I was travelling around the Arabic states for a *National*

Geographic story on Arabian seas. In my diving in Kuwait, Qatar, Oman and UAE I felt the antiquity of the region. A Persian painting from the sixteenth century depicts Alexander the Great being lowered into the sea in a glass bathysphere in order to see what lies beneath the waves. The desire to know the world has ancient roots. I saw much that was new and strange to my eyes. Had the legendary Scheherazade known the richness of Arabia's seas, I wrote in the *Geographic*, she would have had stories for another thousand-and-one nights.

In the estuarine labyrinth of Bubiyan Island, at the head of the Persian Gulf, I found fish called mudskippers that live largely out of the water. Their name in Arabic means 'lazy one', because they appear to be too lethargic to follow the falling tide. Instead, each goggle-eyed fish builds and patrols its own mud-rimmed swimming pool. Shining in slippery coats of sludge, they wriggle through the slurry of their ponds or waddle along the walls on their broad pectoral fins. Occasionally, as if responding to some internal biological necessity, they fling themselves bodily into the air, exuberant as porpoises.

On Masirah Island, off the east coast of Oman, I visited a beach one night to watch hundreds of ghost crabs excavating their burrows and using the spoil to build perfectly conical sand turrets up to 30 centimetres tall. Each crab has one pincer larger than the other. In some it is the right pincer, in some the left. To construct their miniature Mount Fujis they carry a clump of sand between their big pincer on one side and their small pincer plus two walking legs on the other. In the initial stage of construction they spend a lot of time compacting the foundation, thumping the ground with each pincer alternately, as if using a soil compactor. They climb the mountain as they build, eventually standing at the very top to place the last grains of sand.

It is the males who engage in these construction feats, the purpose of which is to impress females: the higher the mound, the more capacious the burrow for egg-laying. But the turrets are ephemeral. Wind and tide level the sand, and next evening the doughty crustaceans must build their turrets afresh.

I travelled to Salalah, in southern Oman, to witness a phenomenon seen nowhere else in the world. Here the reefs of Dhofar flourish as coral gardens during winter and seaweed forests during summer. The trigger for this yin–yang ecological shift is the onset of the khareef, the southwesterly monsoon that bathes the coasts of Yemen and Oman in an upwelling of cold water. Seaweed, dormant in the warm months, responds to the cooler conditions with a burst of luxuriant growth, carpeting the reefs with green, red and golden fronds.

Far more than its reefs, Salalah is famous for frankincense. The city is said to be the perfume capital of Arabia. I was taken to see frankincense groves by Mohsin Musallem Al Amri, who was working for the Environment Society of Oman on a project on sustainable harvesting of the resin — when to cut, how often, which stands are the most productive. A friend of his, Ahmed Salem, a teacher on holiday, joined us. We walked among the trees, some starting to put on spring leaves, others still bare. The bark is paper thin and flakes off in fragrant peels. Mohsin said the trees don't have rings, so they can't be aged that way, but some are believed to be several hundred years old.

Herodotus, the historian of ancient Greece, was so taken by the perfumes of southern Arabia that he said 'the whole country exhales a more than earthly fragrance'. In Salalah that is no exaggeration. Street braziers burn sticks of fragrant wood that fill the air with sweet smoke. I stepped into a perfume shop to buy frankincense. The shopkeeper immediately lit a piece of charcoal, placed aromatic woodchips on the ember for me to enjoy, and dabbed my wrists with fragrant oils. In many Arabian homes, clothes are placed on racks near incense braziers to absorb the fragrance, and women waft their hair with incense smoke — a fragrant fumigation.

This attention to olfactory beauty was just one of the features of Arabic culture that I admired. Another was an impulse to hospitality that I was told arises from a Koranic injunction to welcome strangers. Ahmed was one who showed this kindness. He happened to be a keen diver, and since school was in recess he offered to take me to see the Dhofar reefs.

As we drove out of the city I noticed that camels crossing the four-lane main highway have the right of way. 'Consider the camel,' I told myself. They walk to the beat of their padded feet, hurrying for no man. They seem a quintessentially Islamic animal, as if they might be saying, 'Inshallah, we will find grazing soon, and water.' The look on their faces speaks of infinite patience and acceptance.

Ahmed reached the dive site, but it was the beginning of the khareef and an onshore wind had stirred up the sea, reducing visibility to a few metres. We dived nonetheless, and I saw on the coral-studded rocks the beginnings of kelp growth that would soon flourish in the cooling seas. I had the sense of witnessing an underwater changing of the seasons.

'I am the sea. In my depths all treasures dwell. Have they asked the divers about my pearls?' the Egyptian poet Hafez Ibrahim wrote a century ago. As I explored the seas of

Arabia I felt dwarfed by the exploits of these champions of the sea, the pearl divers of generations past. Forty, fifty, a hundred times a day they dropped to the seafloor, as deep as 20 metres, using a stone to get them down and a rope to raise them back up. They dived without goggles and wore a thin woven garment to protect against jellyfish stings.

With other creatures they took their chances. Men died from stingray jabs, from poisonous stonefish spines, from shark bites. Clownfish — a cruel joke — attacked their eyes as they groped about for oysters. Their eardrums burst, and some went blind from constant exposure to the salty water.

It was hellish work for a heavenly prize. Pearls were the diamonds of the sea. In Hafiz's time they were the Persian Gulf's most valuable resource, and 70,000 men were engaged in collecting them. But the divers saw little of the wealth they generated. The oysters they brought up were thrown into a common pile, to be opened the next day, when dead. Even if a diver brought up a pearl of Steinbeckian magnificence, he would never know it.

Debt drove them to dive. Debt inherited from their fathers and their father's fathers. Debt no diver could hope to discharge. 'O ya mal,' they sang mournfully, 'O money.'

Some of this I learned from a museum of pearl diving in Kuwait City. There I saw the one-piece diver's garment, precursor to the wetsuit, the turtleshell nose clamps they used, leather gloves that protected their fingers. I learned that among the crew on each pearling boat was a full-time singer, and that the Arabic word for pearl is 'lulu', the origin of the girl's name.

I was told that a few of these old-time divers were still alive, so I visited a number of fishermen's clubs trying to find one. The clubs were typically spacious rooms with sofas and cushions on all sides, where men in immaculate dishdasha robes and patterned head scarves read newspapers, played Turkish draughts and talked. Whenever my guide and I entered one of these clubs, we were immediately brought tiny glass cups of cinnamon tea, bottles of iced water, often a bowl of dates, and thick, black, sweet cardamom coffee. Such hospitality is considered common courtesy in Arabia, and I encountered it everywhere.

I never found the old pearl divers, but I came to appreciate that pearling was a matter of deep cultural pride, part of a maritime tradition that was as Arabian as deserts and dates. Until the 1930s, great Kuwaiti dhows, or boums, with names like *The Triumph of Righteousness* and *The Light of the Earth and Sea*, set their lateen sails to the billowing northeasterly wind that blew them to Zanzibar and Mangalore. Months later, the khareef brought them home again. The seasonal fluctuation of the winds was the fuel of Arabian commerce. The winds were Allah's, and the winds were free.

Then came oil, and a seafaring way of life that had endured for millennia melted away at the arrival of a new monetary lord. Oil became the genie that granted the wishes of modernisation and affluence. In just 40 years Arabia was transformed — from camels to Cadillacs, mud houses to hyper-malls — as its citizens rode the magic carpet of petro-wealth.

Environmental concerns were temporarily set aside, especially those of the sea. The shipbuilding industry disappeared. Dhows came out of fibreglass moulds, and were vastly outnumbered by small, fast skiffs, the modern fisher's (and smuggler's) vessel of choice.

At remote fishing ports I saw these skiffs lined up at the daily fish auction, bows pointing to the launching ramp, catches arrayed on deck as neatly as if they were set out for a photo shoot. Some fishers had coral reef fish, some tuna, some a flat John Dory type of fish, some tiny sharks, so small they looked as if they had just been pulled out of their mother's body. On one boat I saw a rare guitarfish.

In Muscat, Dawood Al Wahaïbi, a fisheries consultant and founder of a marine environmental consultancy, explained that unregulated skiff fishing is one of the main causes of Arabia's impoverished seas. He said that in Oman alone there were 20,000 registered fishing skiffs, and probably the same number of unregistered vessels. They are landing fish along a largely unpatrolled 3000 kilometres of coastline. What chance did fish stocks have under such conditions?

Too many human hands are reaching too deep into Arabia's seas and taking more treasure than the sea can possibly replenish. In 2009, a group of leading marine scientists described Arabia's most strategic waterway, the Persian (or Arabian) Gulf, as 'a sea in decline', bedevilled by 'a storm of harmful influences'. Unsustainable fishing, incessant seabed dredging and massive coastal modification were crippling marine ecosystems, they wrote. 'If current trends continue,' they warned, 'we will lose a unique marine environment.'

A moment of truth came in 2004, when the 80,000 or so bottlenose dolphins that normally enter the Arabian Gulf failed to do so. Fingers were pointed at the gargantuan construction project of the Palms and Dubai World, a series of artificial islands and peninsulas off the coast of Dubai. The dolphins' usual migration takes them from the Indian subcontinent, through the Arabian Gulf and then to Somalia and South Africa. Their failure to arrive in the gulf meant collapse for many parts of the marine ecosystem that rely on leftovers from dolphin feeding.

Then, in 2009, a bloom of red algae occurred unlike any that had been seen before. It reached to 27 metres deep. 'If I hadn't had a dive computer with a light I wouldn't have been able to see how deep I was,' my Omani dive guide told me. 'Imagine diving in this,' he said, pointing to a crimson colour in the tablecloth where we were sitting. 'Fish were floating upside down. Urchins were sick and had lost all their spines. Coral was bleached, completely deoxygenated.'

One of the groups at greatest risk is sharks. Of all the insults to Arabia's marine life, none is more grotesque than the mountain of shark carcasses that arrives nightly in the Deira fish market in Dubai, trucked from landing sites around Oman and the Emirates, from there to make its way east — a stinking tide of fins and flesh.

I met Rima Jabado, a doctoral student at United Arab Emirates University, conspicuous in her yellow rubber boots and hot pink top as she moved through the market counting and measuring hammerheads, threshers, silkies, makos and bulls — the thoroughbreds of Arabian seas, carted here to be hocked off like horsemeat. Totemic animals that divers dream of encountering underwater are hauled out of the back of trucks with meat hooks and lined up on the pavement, grimy and bloodied, row upon row of scowling mouths.

An auctioneer worked his way along the line, followed by a retinue of buyers calculating profit margins on their smartphones. In their wake a man expertly severed the fins and laid them out on plastic tarps for separate sale. A pickup truck pulled up, and the driver unloaded a dozen sacks of dried fins. He plunged his hands into a sack and lifted out handfuls of small grey triangles, stiff as plywood. There must have been several thousand fins in this one shipment.

'When I started working here, I thought "That's a lot of sharks",' Rima told me. 'But when you see it every day, you think, How is this possible? How can this last?'

As we walked and talked a muezzin gave the evening call to prayer from a mosque whose minarets made artful silhouettes against a golden sky. Across the carpark, the retail fish market was crowded with Emirati housewives gliding down aisles of laden stalls, passing their purchases to Pakistani houseboys to be wheeled in garden barrows to a rank of waiting SUVs.

An old name for this part of Arabia was the Pirate Coast. Trading ships carried companies of archers to repel thieves. But how to solve the plunder of the sea itself?

Rima travels the length of the Emirates coast, from Abu Dhabi to Ras Al Khaimah, tallying sharks and interviewing fishermen. Everywhere it is the same story: catches are down, and fishing intensity is up.

One of the questions she asks the fishermen is whether they think sharks should be protected. Some say, 'No, why should we protect them? Sharks are a gift from God. He will replenish them.' Others say that sharks should be protected, but that it needs to happen across the region. 'If we protect them here, do you think the Iranians are going to stop taking them?' they tell her. 'Why should I stop fishing for sharks and miss out on revenue if some other person keeps taking them?'

Eight countries border the gulf. 'They have the same kind of culture and heritage, speak the same language, face the same problems and share the same resources,' Rima says. 'But there is not one unified management system. There is not one single thing that they agree on. Why aren't they working together?'

Her concerns run deeper than fisheries management. The impact of an environmental disaster in so shallow and enclosed a waterway is appalling to contemplate. There are many hundreds of oil and gas platforms in the gulf, and tens of thousands of tanker movements annually through the Strait of Hormuz. 'What if there was a *Deepwater Horizon* event here?' she asks. 'The average depth of the gulf is 30 metres. One big spill could wipe out whole marine ecosystems.'

On the island of Masirah, a six-hour drive and ferry trip from Muscat, I saw how unregulated fishing affects other marine life. I was there to meet turtle researcher Andy Wilson and learn about his work with loggerhead turtles. Masirah, 65 kilometres long, 16 kilometres wide and vaguely ant-shaped, is one the most important nesting islands for this species, but in 30 years the number of turtles coming to the island to nest has declined by 80 per cent.

Andy spends a lot of time searching Masirah's sandy beaches for the remaining 20 per cent. Often what he finds isn't pleasant. 'I see a lot of death,' he told me.

Night is the best time to see turtles coming ashore. As we approached the island's eastern beaches on a scouting drive, he switched off the vehicle's headlights and covered the dashboard instruments. Turtles sometimes walk up to a kilometre inland to dig a nest, he said. Streetlights, building lights and vehicle lights can disorient them. If they are out of the water for more than a few hours they will overheat and die.

There are other more immediate threats for the animals to contend with. Andy pointed out the floats of a four-kilometre-long fishing net that had been set just beyond the breakers. It seemed incredible — a fishing net next to a turtle nesting beach.

Andy saw a patch of phosphorescence in the water and

a round shape on the sand, and switched on a red light to investigate. It was a dead loggerhead. We drove on and found more dead loggerheads and a hawksbill. Each was bloated, mouth open in rictus. Andy said these turtles had died in a single fishing episode: caught in nets, then cut free and dumped.

These are Andy's Arabian nights.

We rose next morning at dawn so that he could measure, photograph and take biopsy samples of the dead turtles we had seen. As we drove along the beach we found a loggerhead in her nest, not moving. Having seen so many dead turtles, Andy thought this one was also dead, but then she blinked. He figured she had become exhausted, and by the look of her criss-crossing tracks she seemed to have walked a long way before finally finding a nest site to her liking. She appeared to have completed egg laying, and had filled the nest chamber with sand. We waited to see if she would return to the sea. Apart from a big sticky tear that fell from one of her eyes and the movement of her throat as she breathed, she was motionless. Andy went to the Land Cruiser for a couple of bottles of mineral water and poured one over the head of the turtle. This produced an instant reaction. She clambered out of the hollow in the sand and started heading for the sea. With a few stops to rest, she lumbered steadily seaward, until the waves received her.

No animals speak to me of antiquity as turtles do. As they broach the shore and heave their heavy selves to dry sand above the reach of spring tides, as they flick sand one languid flipper at a time, laboriously excavating a nest, as they extrude the sticky white eggs, as they cover the nest again — all this slow-motion activity seems to have been pre-programmed in ancient times, a ritual handed down by ancestors.

Marine turtles have existed on the planet for more than 200 million years. Yet their light is flickering out. Not one of the seven species is secure. I met many people in Arabia who felt the indictment of such a situation on a culture that was shaped by the sea. Dawood was one. 'Dhows took our fathers and grandfathers across the Indian Ocean,' he said. 'We had no fear of the sea. Now we have lost our connection to those traditions, and it makes me feel sad and sour. We are heading into a dark place: in seeking financial gain we are suffering ecological loss.'

Others spoke wistfully of the pearlers, who managed the pearl resource sustainably for generations. 'They were better people. They had better values. They worked together.'

They spoke of the Bedu and other nomadic tribes, who understood the need to prepare ahead for unfavourable future conditions. They understood precaution. 'We had something precious, the Bedouin culture, but it is fading,' one man told me. 'Dubai is now a society where you have to consume as much as possible, then get back into line and consume again.'

I thought of the words the poet Khalil Gibran wrote in 1923: that Arabia was an old man who had lost his teeth, and also an infant who had yet to sprout them.

But there are inklings of that sprouting: a growing sense of marine stewardship across the region, and perhaps a more unified approach to preserving the riches of the sea. Several gulf states have given legal protection to the whale shark. The giant filter-feeder has been turning up in unexpected places. In 2009 a Dubai-based whale shark researcher, David Robinson, was startled when a Google image search turned up a photograph of a pod of whale sharks among the drilling platforms of Al Shaheen, a major oil and gas field off the coast of Qatar.

'The photograph was on the Facebook page of a worker on a gas rig. I sent him a message, he added me as a friend, and now we're getting a stream of pictures from him and others,' Robinson said. 'In fact, most of my sightings are coming through Facebook. In one photograph I counted 150 animals. I'd like to say we discovered the sharks through tirelessly scouring the oceans, but that would be a lie. It was through scouring the oceans of cyberspace! Science by Facebook — a bit embarrassing, really.'

The discovery of whale sharks in Al Shaheen has led to other discoveries there. Seasonal mass spawning of lobsters has been observed, with the lobsters rising to the surface at night — perhaps attracted by the gas flares — and turning the sea into a vast crustacean soup. With fishing banned and boat traffic restricted in many oil and gas fields, these areas likely serve as de facto marine reserves. The platforms themselves may act as giant fish-aggregating devices.

They seemed to be doing that job when I dived with Robinson at Al Shaheen. With a flare stack belching flame overhead, I watched a shoal of jacks circle the legs of the platform and spinner dolphins launch their lissome bodies into the air. A hammerhead cruised at the edge of visibility, finding sanctuary within the ring of fire.

Other manifestations of marine guardianship are appearing. In Kuwait, hundreds of keen amateur divers have formed the ecological equivalent of SWAT teams, dedicated to repairing the environmental damage of war and waste. They lift sunken vessels from the seabed and remove tonnes of snared fishing nets from Kuwait's coral reefs.

I travelled with three of these divers to the island of Qaruh, a tiny sand cay 40 kilometres off the Kuwaiti coast, with a few buildings and a cellphone tower on it. We were an odd assortment of reef repairers, including a computer engineer, a television producer and a former leader of Kuwait's grand mosque. As we drove south to the boat harbour the men spoke about the complexities of implementing fishing regulations when enforcers and officials are so closely connected socially with those they are supposed to police. They also spoke of the traditional commitment to family, community and tribe, which can seem more important than a commitment to environmental law, and that this also undermines the authority of the enforcement regime.

Qaruh is derived from the Arabic word for tar. As we approached the island there was a strong smell of oil from natural underwater seeps, and when the boat stopped, patches of slick floated past on the current. Dragonflies were flying around the boat and landing on us. A big one landed on my face, its legs prickling my skin. The men said something about dragonflies bringing good luck.

I made my first dive with Dari Al Huwail, who was monitoring coral health for the Coral Watch project. He used a card printed with swatches of various shades of brown and green, noting the maximum and minimum colour density for each coral colony and recording it on a tablet. I spent the dive in my usual reverie of coral-reef enchantment, watching blue-striped fish darting among the black spines of sea urchins.

When I surfaced, the other divers said they had found a fishing net snagged on staghorn coral, and invited me to help cut it away. The nightmare of knotted nylon meshes yielded reluctantly to our collection of chef's knives and garden shears.

It felt good to make a small contribution to the restoration of Arabia's reef health.

There had been an earlier occasion when I felt a similar satisfaction. I was diving in a coral maze near the Strait of Hormuz and came across an abandoned fish trap, like a large, dome-shaped, wire-mesh lobster pot. Inside were four bumblebee-striped bannerfish and an Arabian surgeonfish, whose sleek black fins and tail seemed rimmed by blue fire. The scene was as incongruous as coming upon a cage of parrots in the Amazon rainforest.

Fish traps — gargoor — are deployed in their tens of thousands around Arabia's coasts. You see them being made at every port. This one had come adrift and wedged itself in the reef. The surgeonfish (so named for a pair of razor-sharp orange 'scalpels' near the tail, used in territorial jousting) was butting its head against the mesh, trying to get out. I reached inside the trap's funnel opening, grasped the slime-covered wires and everted the thing. The corroding mesh tore in my hands, leaving a hole large enough for the fish to escape. I swam around the other side and herded them to freedom.

That small Samaritan moment was inconsequential except to me. The removal of nets from coral reefs could be seen as similarly inconsequential, but multiply each rescue by a hundred, then a thousand, then ten thousand, and perhaps they amount to a changed attitude towards the sea.

We surfaced and rested for a while, ate Arabic flatbreads filled with haloumi and drank minted yoghurt. We dived again, and when we surfaced we noticed a dust storm forming on the horizon. As we returned from the island, crossing a sea as smooth as a saucer of milk, two of the team found space among the scuba gear on deck to pray. Ignoring the symphonic thunder

of twin 200-horsepower outboards, they prostrated their
bodies and uttered the ancient words of invocation and praise,
giving voice to the hope that good might come to the world.

At the other end of the gulf, in Dubai, public-spirited
beachgoers are expressing that hope by collecting
stranded turtles and taking them to a rehabilitation facility
domiciled in the Burj Al Arab hotel. While diners consume king
crab and quaff Moët beside the hotel's million-litre aquarium,
behind the plexiglass walls hawksbill turtles convalesce in
bubbling tanks. In 2011, the year I was there, 350 juvenile
turtles were being cared for, many of them victims of 'cold
stunning' — metabolic inertia caused by the drop in sea
temperature caused by the khareef.

To recuperate, they need little more than a stable environment,
a course of antibiotics and regular feeding, explained Warren
Baverstock, the aquarium operations manager, as we walked along
a line of tanks. We paused periodically to scratch the backs of the
splashing turtles. The animals twisted their necks and flippers in
pleasure at the attention. 'If they survive the first 24 hours, there is
a 99 per cent chance they will recover,' he said.

Baverstock told me a curious thing. Even inside a windowless
building, the turtles always know where the sea is. 'They swim up
and down the wall nearest the sea, lifting their heads up, looking
for it.'

Mass releases of the rehabilitated turtles are staged at
nearby beaches to publicise the work and reinforce the
message that Arabia's marine life is valuable, vulnerable
and in need of protection. Each turtle is implanted with a
microchip for identification. Baverstock said that in the seven

years the project had been operating, no turtle had ever washed ashore twice.

The hotel's most famous patient was an adult green turtle given the name Dibba, which arrived with a fractured skull. Baverstock and his team needed 18 months to rehabilitate the turtle, but Dibba, released with a satellite transmitter glued to its carapace, repaid its caregivers with a 259-day, 8000-kilometre migratory journey, looping down the Arabian Sea, passing the Maldives, skirting Sri Lanka and reaching as far as the Andaman Islands before the transmitter battery failed.

Dibba traced an ancient route imprinted not just on turtles but on the cultural memory of Arabia's peoples. This way came the dhows laden with Basra dates and pearls. This way they returned, carrying camphor, silks, sandalwood and cloves. Every Arabian family had its sea captains and sailors, its pearl divers and boat carpenters, a saltwater legacy written in its genes.

Modernity has dimmed that memory. 'We have lost the thirst for the sea that can only be quenched by going to the sea,' Dawood told me with sadness in his eyes. Yet for others the thirst is returning. Increasing numbers of Arabs are going to the sea not to exploit it but to experience it as it is. They are renewing their bond with ancient shores and rediscovering the poet's truth: 'In my depths all treasures dwell.'

The inland sea

ALMOST ALL MY UNDERWATER exploration has been in salt water, with one spectacular exception: a *National Geographic* assignment in the Okavango Delta in Botswana. I spent several weeks over two seasons in that remarkable wetland, a sea of papyrus and waterlilies, of tinkling frogs and bellowing hippos, of somnolent crocodiles and soaring cranes.

Some of those weeks I spent in the company of my photographer friends David Doubilet and Jennifer Hayes. Guiding us were Brad Bestelink and Andy Crawford, a husband-and-wife team who are now filmmakers in their own right.

National Geographic had published stories about the delta before, but none with an underwater perspective, and for good reason: the delta is home to a healthy population of Nile crocodiles, which regularly reach the length of two people lying end to end. Males can weigh a tonne. The teeth of a fully grown adult are as big as thumbs, and their bite force is unsurpassed in the animal kingdom.

Previous writers and photographers had preferred not to place themselves in the same water as these aggressive and calculating predators. People told us that crocodiles are one of the few predators that will surveil humans and strategise how to harvest them. They told us we were mad to tempt fate by going underwater. Did we have a death wish?

The baYei people, one of several Okavango tribes, teach their children a poem: 'I am the river. My surface gives you life. Below is death.' For David and me, going below was an essential part of our work. We wanted to see the delta as few had dared to see it before — a croc's-eye view.

We believed that by diving in winter we were minimising the risk. The big, cold-blooded reptiles' metabolisms would be sluggish in the cooler temperatures, we conjectured. They would be more inclined to bask on land than bother with two-legged interlopers in the water.

As a precaution, we would also keep away from the main channels where adult crocodiles reside, and dive in calm, clear side channels and backwaters edged with papyrus and thronged with waterlily pads and their pink, white and blue flowers.

We based ourselves near the aptly named Panhandle, where the Okavango River enters the fan-shaped, pan-shaped delta. It was the season of the annual flood. Generated by rainfall 800 kilometres and two countries away in the highlands of Angola, the flood snakes down the Okavango River and spreads across the delta, filling its lagoons and channels and spilling outwards to inundate the floodplains.

This part of southern Africa is so flat that the flood takes three months to reach the delta, and four more to traverse its 240-kilometre length. Yet by the time its force is spent, the flood has increased the Okavango's wetland area threefold, creating an oasis the size of Marlborough at the edge of the Kalahari Desert. In a land withered by drought, this gift of water is like unction, and all nature responds to it.

The flood peaks at the Panhandle in April, raising the level of the Okavango River by 2 metres. By late June, when we arrived, the level was dropping. Sediment borne on the flood tide had settled, and the water in Nxamaseri channel was clean and clear.

I came to love that channel with its waterlily margins across which African jacanas, known as lilytrotters, picked their way, dipping the lily pads beneath the surface with each long-toed step. Beyond the waterlilies, broad stands of papyrus stretched to the horizon, their pompom heads turned fiery red in the Okavango's blazing dawns and dusks. Wild date palms leaned over the water, weaverbird nests dangling from their fronds like Christmas-tree ornaments. On drier ground stood tall knobthorn trees, their upper branches festooned with crimson-flowered mistletoe, and shady jackalberry trees, whose sweet, soft fruit tastes like loquats.

In backwater eddies, congregations of whirligig beetles danced on the mirror surface. Malachite kingfishers, jewels of the Okavango, swooped from one reed perch to another in iridescent flashes. Damselflies darted between waterlily flowers, seeking mates. We found one pair engaged in amphibious coupling, one above, one below the water. Air bubbles trapped between the cuticle hairs of the underwater partner shone like drops of mercury on its turquoise body. A fishing spider, patience personified, watched and waited. These arachnids use their two back legs to anchor themselves to a lily pad and deploy the front six in the water. When a minnow comes within range, the spider grasps and sinks its fangs into the fish, delivering the poisonous coup de grâce. Baby crocodiles half a metre long rested with their snouts out of the water among the lily pads.

Diving at Nxamaseri was like swimming in a salad bowl. Plants with bronze, gold and green leaves, all richly veined with burgundy, created lush lettuce beds on the sand. Candyfloss wisps of algae wafted in the current and formed dense, smothering pillows where the water was still. Glittering topminnows with turquoise eyes shoaled through a jungle of waterlily stems that rose from the buried tubers to the leaves and flowers, floating metres above.

Waterlilies have a clever way of bringing their flowers back underwater once they have been fertilised, so that the seeds are released below the surface. The stems, which have stood straight while they held the flowers aloft, start to coil into a helix, dragging the flowers under. The flowers ripen into fruit that eventually disintegrates, releasing a frogspawn of seeds into the water.

Waterlily stems are hollow and make good drinking straws. Wherever I travelled in the delta I made sure to snap one off and suck up a deep draft, mindful of the saying, 'He who drinks of the water of the Okavango will always return.' I wanted to give myself every chance.

In deeper parts of the channel the light became bottle-green, the water pellucid and mysterious. Bream and tigerfish — the latter named for their mouthful of needle-sharp teeth — schooled past the limbs of drowned trees. A hippo skull lay partly sunk in the pale silt. Little giraffe-patterned fish called squeakers — named for the sound they make when caught — sheltered in the eye sockets.

Nearby, the hull of a mokoro — the traditional dugout canoe of the baYei people — lay on its side, its voyaging days over. Purple crabs peeked out from the narrow gap between its hull and the channel bed, while squeakers browsed upside down on green algal fuzz, their sensory barbels tapping and probing like a blind person's cane. This is their normal mode; they belong to a group known as upside-down catfish.

Something white caught the light. I picked it up: a crocodile tooth. Nxamaseri villagers had told of a fisherman who had gone out recently and not returned. Was the mokoro his? More to the point, was the owner of this tooth still in the vicinity?

As we motored to our dive sites, we often passed large crocodiles basking on the riverbanks in well-used haulouts, usually with chutes down which they slid into the water if disturbed. Some lay with their mouths open, a behaviour once fancifully thought to allow cleaner birds to pick meat from between their teeth, but now considered an aid in regulating body temperature. At night, when the air grew cool, the warmth-loving crocs floated among the papyrus and reeds at the water's edge. Their eyes gleamed red in our spotlight as we idled along the channel.

One night I slipped into the water to observe a 2-metre crocodile that had submerged as our boat approached. Pulling myself through a tangle of waterlilies, I reached a position directly above the animal, then dived down for a closer look. Magnificent! — the vivid black-on-fawn markings; the two lines of upraised scutes on the back, merging into the serrated keel of the tail, jagged as a ripsaw; the gorgeously veined irises of the unblinking eyes; teeth like a white zipper. I was only an arm's length from the animal, and my nervous system was awash with the adrenalin of the moment.

The crocodile moved. I followed it through the underwater foliage, playing my torch beam on its squat, muscular legs.

Then, with a scything flick of its tail, it sped away into the darkness.

Although crocodiles are the delta's most feared predator, locals said that hippopotamuses cause more deaths and injuries. Accidental meetings in narrow channels are often the trigger for an altercation. Hippos can bite a canoe in half with one snap of their jaws, and their tusks can puncture an aluminium boat as if it were a beer can. The 2-tonne vegetarians aren't slowpokes, either. Guy Lobjoit, an Okavango fishing guide, told me he once had a hippo keep up with him while he was doing 40 kilometres an hour in his runabout. 'The boat was planing, and this thing was pushing up a bow-wave right next to me,' he said. 'Gave my ticker a bit of a flutter.'

We sometimes heard them at night, cropping grass near the camp. During the day we watched them socialise, blowing and bobbing, sometimes heaving their bulk out of the water and splashing colossally back down.

David yearned to take close-up underwater photographs of hippos, something that had never been done. *National Geographic*'s engineering department had made a radio-controlled raft for one of David's underwater camera rigs, and sent an engineer out to the delta with us to operate and troubleshoot the contraption. We gathered one morning at the edge of a pool where a dozen or more hippos were resting. The raft was deployed and steered towards the lounging animals. Its tiny electric motor whined like a mosquito. We wondered what would happen. Would the hippos tolerate a mechanical intruder in their midst? Or would one of them simply open its jaws and crush it? Neither. As the camera approached the hippos departed. They had no interest in us or our technologies. Perhaps for some animals curiosity has no evolutionary advantage. Although he tried several more times, David never did get the hippo shots he hoped for.

I wanted to experience the delta as traditional Okavangans do, so I made an overnight camping trip with two baYei: an older man known as Madala — 'old one' — and a young fishing guide called Fish.

Fish poled a mokoro made from kiaat, a teak-like timber, with metal patches covering cracks, which he called its wounds. Madala poled a plastic canoe. He said he preferred plastic canoes because they are more stable than a mokoro.

Poling is a hypnotically beautiful way to travel. Each thrust of the wooden pole moves the mokoro through beds of reed and sedge that whisper against the hull. Grasshoppers and emerald leaf beetles jumped onto our clothes and then jumped off again. I trailed my fingers in the warm water and studied the microcosmos of waterstriders, backswimmers, beetles, and frogs no bigger than a fingernail. The foghorn snort of a hippo warned us to avoid its channel. A herd of red lechwe, a species of antelope with long hooves adapted for swamp travel, splashed away at full gallop when we came into view.

As we ghosted along, stopping here and there at wooded islands, Fish pointed to various plants and described their properties. The root of the star apple makes an excellent toothbrush; the bark of the rain tree can be ground up and thrown into the water to paralyse fish; chewed sicklebush leaves are good for treating snake bite.

We talked quietly, hoping to see a sitatunga, another antelope adapted for marsh living. Fish stopped poling and whispered, 'Sitatunga coming this way.' We saw a big male feeding near a palm-covered island. He spotted us and bolted away. A few moments later he gave a barking alarm call, like clearing his throat. When sitatunga are threatened, they sink down into the water until only their nostrils breach the surface.

We heard a bird that speaks its own name: 'I . . . am . . . a red-eyed dove. I . . . am . . . a red-eyed dove.' We heard a hadeda ibis calling — another bird that repeats its name, with long, noisy calls that sound like complaints. Madala said that if the baYei hear a hadeda 'they know maybe some dangerous animal is nearby or maybe some people are coming to fight them'. Conversely, when they hear the cardinal woodpecker's laughter they know that something is coming to make them happy. 'Maybe your family will be eating a big meal tonight.'

On an island burned by a lightning strike we crept over the ash-covered soil, through spiky palm stalks, towards a wattled crane, its white, S-shaped neck delicately extended, ready to probe into the shallows.

Madala cut a tall papyrus stem and pounded the fleshy white base against his palm to soften it before handing it to me to eat. It was sweet, fibrous and refreshing, reminiscent of fresh coconut. What I enjoyed most about it was the thought that I am a writer eating paper.

He gave me the rubbery pith of bulrush to try — Okavango chewing gum, it's called — and pulled up waterlily fruit for cooking later. He cut the stem of a young date palm, removed the outer leaf bases and extracted the central white pith. It tasted like raw macadamia.

We made camp under the boughs of a sycamore fig. While Madala set his net in a lagoon thick with waterlilies, Fish waded into the floodplain to spear small fish with a porcupine quill. It's a technique small boys learn, along with such tricks as sticking a thorn into a poison-apple fruit to make a spinning top. I climbed a baobab tree to collect its maraca-shaped fruits which contain a white pulp that substitutes well for cream of tartar. Madala mixed the pulp with water to make a tangy sauce.

That night we rolled balls of maize-meal porridge — 'mealie meal' or pap — with our fingers and dipped them in a casserole of freshly caught bream and waterlily fruit, with sides of boiled date-palm pith and baobab milk. In the firelight Madala told stories about the baYei people. To keep the mosquitoes at bay, Fish lit a football-sized lump of elephant dung which smoked aromatically for hours.

We heard lions in the distance, and I thought of Laurens van der Post's observation that the lion's roar 'is to silence what the shooting star is to the dark of the night'. The frog chorus rose and fell, though the effect was spoiled by a group of French tourists on a neighbouring island singing 'Frère Jacques' at the top of their voices.

Other than the presence of a few tourists and a carton of long-life milk for our Five Roses tea, I suspected that little in this scene had changed since the first European explorers visited the Okavango more than 150 years ago.

I travelled deeper into the delta with Adrian Dandridge, a guide from a family with deep roots in Okavango. We motored through a maze of channels flanked and often choked with papyrus. The delta would not be what it is if not for *Cyperus papyrus*, the paper reed. Each year, when the flood arrives, it brings a load of suspended sand and salts. Papyrus acts as a water filter, trapping sand around its fibrous base, causing the riverbed to rise. It also traps organic matter, building up a layer of peat.

The collective acquisition of sand and peat raises the riverbed above the surrounding floodplain, causing water to seep sideways through the fringing stands of papyrus and reeds. As the bed continues to rise, less water flows along the channel and more leaks sideways. Clumps of papyrus (which are not rooted in the soil but linked together in floating mats) break off and jam the channel until, like a clogged artery, it becomes completely blocked.

At this point the hippo comes to the aid of the delta's circulatory system, breaking through papyrus jams and forming new channel connections. It is only because the delta is so flat (a gradient of about a hundredth of a degree) that water follows such randomly created corridors. The path of least resistance turns out to be the path the hippos have trod. The old channels are left standing high and dry above the surrounding marshes and become long, sinuous islands that are colonised by riverine forest.

This fluidity in the landscape is, in fact, what sustains the delta as a living organism. Channel switching prevents the accumulation of salts in any one part of the delta and stops the whole thing from becoming terminally saline, which was the fate of the Makgadikgadi Pans, a vast, parched set of salt pans southeast of the delta.

Papyrus the channel-blocker is also an island-builder in its own right. Decomposition of its dead stalks results in beds of peat up to 4 metres thick. When these beds catch fire, they leave ash deposits that become the foundation of still more islands. Exploring the delta's labyrinth of channels is thus a lesson in ecology as much as geography, and an invitation to reflect on the constancy of change. Everything here is in a state of becoming. Nothing is quite as it was last time you visited. Channels that were clear last week might be blocked today. Adrian must periodically climb a tree to get a view of the way ahead.

Negotiating mats of floating papyrus stalks calls for a particular delta skill. The driver approaches the blockage at speed, one hand on the outboard, which he lifts at the last instant. The motor screams as the propeller spins in air. If the driver has timed it right, momentum will carry the boat over the papyrus raft and into clear water on the other side.

We camped under waterberry trees and spent the next day on what Adrian called a crawling safari. Our interest was not in the delta's charismatic megafauna but in its humbler denizens. Adrian pointed out a water mongoose midden, hyena droppings, a fish eagle nest, the remains of an otter's meal and the massive nest of a hamerkop, a relative of the pelican. Its Afrikaans name, meaning 'hammerhead', refers to a crest on the back of its head.

There is a deep African fascination with divining which creatures have passed by before you. Adrian referred to creatures as people, often wondering aloud what these people had been doing in the places we were now exploring. He grew up in the delta and knows its wildlife as if they are family members. I appreciated this personalisation and respect for the natural world. In Africa, more so than in most places, you have the sense of being a guest. You walk humbly here, perhaps because there are plenty of animals that are larger than you are, or that can kill you. Or is it that there is a genetic memory that humans originated here? That the trees under which we camped could have sheltered distant ancestors?

We passed trees full of roosting great white egrets. We watched African skimmers dance across the water's surface. They have a unique bill, with an enlarged, flattened lower mandible which they dip in the water as they fly: if it touches a fish, the skimmer's bill snaps shut. We snacked on the orange fruit of the African mangosteen, which is mostly seed but has a rime of tart, tasty flesh.

In keeping with the maxim that the least is the greatest of all, one of the largest contributions to the life of the delta is made by some of its smallest inhabitants: termites. It turns out that termites are a lot more than pasty white insects that gnaw on dead plants and manage subterranean fungus farms. Their colonies are giant construction companies that have transformed the Okavango Delta from a piece of flat real estate into a mosaic of more than 150,000 islands.

It all stems from the termites' need for air conditioning. They build above-ground air vents to control the temperature in their underground networks of galleries and tunnels. These turrets, several metres high, and their surrounding earthworks are above flood level. They are also resistant to dissolution. Termites make their mortar from clay particles fused with saliva and a chemical salt. It is said that the clay of the termitarium is harder than any other substrate in the delta.

Termites also concentrate minerals in their mounds, so if the seed of a date palm, fig tree, knobthorn tree or some other woody plant is blown or dropped there it will have a superb growing medium. The mound becomes an embryonic island. As the trees grow, they concentrate salts carried by the floodwater in the soil and groundwater beneath them — a 'toxic waste storage system', as South African geosciences professor Terence McCarthy described it to me.

Trees not only keep the water in the delta fresh but also expand the size of their island platforms through precipitation of those salts, especially of carbonates. Thus what the termites start, the trees continue, engineering not just a landscape but an entire ecosystem.

Termites, hippos and papyrus — these three ecosystem engineers are part of a system so intricate and responsive that I came to regard it as a proxy for the earth itself. Together, they have turned the largest inland delta in the world into a wetland Eden.

The story of the delta is as much about the absence of water as about its presence. The arrival of water from Angola comes in the driest part of the year, when rain is both a fading memory and a distant promise. That seemed to me a kind of miracle. To appreciate the impact of this gift to the land and the wildlife, I travelled southeast across the delta to places not yet reached by the year's advancing tide.

The flood moves on multiple fronts like the columns of an army. It is like a living thing, and locals travel long distances to look for it. It brings out the tracking impulse in a person. I went flood hunting with Brad's father, PJ Bestelink, who runs horse safaris with his wife, Barney, and is deeply knowledgeable about the delta and its wildlife.

The air was still and fiercely hot as we crunched across brittle stalks of dead grass to where a tongue of new water was creeping across the ground at walking speed. PJ seemed animated, energised, enlivened by the water. Perhaps it is only in a drought-prone country and continent that water takes on a preciousness beyond all else. The national greeting, as well as the national currency, in Botswana is the Setswana word for rain — pula.

Stalk by stalk the water advanced, pushing across dry sand, running along paths trampled by elephants and hippos, seeping slowly sideways across the malapo, the floodplain. Tannins in the water give it the colour of draught beer, and it bubbled as it seeped into the dusty hollows and runnels of the soil.

I saw minnows in the vanguard, riding the tongue, swirling along in the current, frontrunners of a spawning horde that would soon turn the floodplain into a fish nursery. As the seeping floodwater soaked into the thatch of dry grass stalks, it triggered an awakening of frogs that had been dormant in the dry conditions. They immediately began calling, some with loud Geiger-counter clicks, others chinking like a chandelier, summoned from their deep mud burrows by the presence of water.

Egrets, blacksmith plovers and red-billed teal kept pace with the water and the life it was conjuring from the desiccated land. From nowhere, pied kingfishers appeared, diving like bolts of rainbow lightning into the channel. Lilac-breasted rollers, Botswana's national bird, hunted for insects flushed out by the bubbling water.

A flock of saddle-billed storks spiralled down like para-chutists. They fly like a bent pin, with the long legs trailing behind and the bill down-pointed. The bill looks like it's been painted in the colours of an electrical resister: red–black–red, with a yellow saddle near the eye. The white wings are magnificently wide.

From the south, a herd of elephants entered the plain, moving like blocks of granite through the tawny grasses. They lumbered towards the widening ribbon of water, trunks cocked in an S, snuffing the sweet elixir. Standing at the water's edge, the thirsty animals sucked up trunkfuls and gushed it into their mouths, spilling barely a drop.

There is a belief that older female elephants hold a matriarchal memory of water. That they could have a clairvoyant's foreknowledge of the flood's arrival wouldn't surprise me. If circumnavigating albatrosses can time their annual arrival at their nesting islands to within a few days, and whales visit feeding grounds ahead of seasonal pulses of abundance, then such a vital event as a flood in a famished landscape could surely become imprinted in the pachyderm psyche.

PJ drove to a lagoon that had filled since the day before. He stepped out of the Land Rover to assess fresh buffalo dung. He studied the tracks and estimated that 20 had drunk here. Locals are extremely wary of buffalo — much more so than they are of elephants, for instance. Buffalo are unpredictable and often aggressive. The only time I observed them at close range was from the safety of a tree Andy and Brad had insisted I climb.

We stopped again to watch a flock of wattled cranes. I counted 130. Their wings are so large they drape behind them like an old-fashioned lady's bustle. American author Peter Matthiessen called his book on cranes *The Birds of Heaven*, and so they seem, an angelic presence. They prance and display on their bamboo-thin legs, then the entire flock lifts into the sky together, honking noisily. They don't flap their wings so much as stroke the air.

I loved the birds of Botswana, as I loved the sound of cowbells and the smell of woodsmoke as I travelled. During the assignment I carried a feather from the lilac-breasted roller in my glasses case. Afterwards I bought a CD of birdcalls of southern Africa so I could listen to the sounds I had grown familiar with. The coucal, with its call like someone blowing over the mouth of a bottle while it is being filled. Pel's fishing owl, with a call described as 'the screeching howl of a lost soul falling into a bottomless pit'. Swamp boubous, which call in pairs: the female makes a clicking sound like castanets, the male chimes in with a low whistle. They do this repeatedly, always in synchrony. Their duetting is thought to strengthen the bond between them.

PJ knew of a large shallow pan that had dried up in the weeks before the flood's arrival, and wanted to investigate. He said that catfish can survive the drying out of a pan by burying themselves in mud. We walked across a sun-crisped stubble of grass and rushes to the centre of the pan, its deepest part. The broken shells of freshwater snails lay bleaching on the ground. Open-billed storks, which have a nutcracker-like gap between the two mandibles of their bills, perfect for crunching these molluscs, had dined well here as the water evaporated.

'We're too late,' said PJ. The mud had turned to cracked clay and was littered with catfish skeletons. Marabou storks, known as undertaker birds because, seen from the back, they seem to be wearing a black cloak, picked among the bones for scraps of flesh. Some of these fish would have weighed 10 kilograms in life. The flood was less than a kilometre away and would soon transform this place into a broad lagoon, but it had not arrived in time to save the catfish from death by dehydration. Their blunt, eyeless skulls underscored the central truth of the delta: water is life.

I wanted to see how Botswanans responded to the arrival of the new water, so I visited Maun, the town that serves as gateway to the delta, and headed up the dry bed of the Thamalakane River, looking for water. Maun means 'place of reeds'. The Batawana people, the dominant delta tribe, chose it as their main settlement site in the late 1800s because of its year-round lushness. But the route that water takes through the delta is in constant flux, and the flow has been shifting westward. The result is that Maun has an acute water shortage. The place of reeds has become a place of dust.

It was a breathless July day, the sky blue as the Botswana flag, the air full of the smell of wild sage. A few kilometres upstream from Maun, I watched as the flood crept along the Thamalakane's parched bed. Children dug furiously with sticks in the sand to encourage the trickle to run faster. Some leaped back and forth across the steadily widening stream, laughing with excitement. Others just let it run over their bare feet, looking at it as if it were the first time they had seen water. 'The water is coming,' I heard a father explain to his daughter. 'The fish are coming. The waterlilies are coming. Life is coming.'

On a bank of the river, behind a twig fence that didn't look as if it could keep out a goat, let alone a cow or a hippo, Flay Million Dube walked around his vegetable plot. With a smile as broad as the straw hat that shaded his eyes, he told me, 'I'm not working today because I'm so happy.' He had just been down to the river to wash his face and hands in the new water, he said. Tomorrow he would put fresh, cool mud around his beds of spinach, broccoli and spring onion. The water was late, he said, but it had come, and that was all that mattered.

In a thatch-roofed bar nearby, Maunites who had driven out from town sipped sundowners and toasted the flood's arrival. 'The English discuss the weather; we discuss the water,' one told me. 'Before it comes, we drink beer and talk about when it will arrive. When it's here, we drink beer and talk about how much has come. When it's gone, we drink beer and feel sad.'

By October, that time of sadness has come. The floodwaters have vanished. The floodplains dry out, and water levels in the channels and lagoons drop to their lowest levels. People cast thirsty glances at the sky, where glowering thunderclouds build in the afternoons, but the summer rains are still two months away. Locals told me they start playing games with the rain gods, trying to provoke rainfall, such as putting chairs outside for a braai, hanging out washing, planning a fishing trip, hoping the gods will smite them with a deluge.

As the delta shrinks, life retreats. Fish born in the floodplains when the water was high withdraw to the permanent channels, and this influx of flesh triggers an Okavango phenomenon: the catfish run. Sharp-toothed catfish, locally called barbels — the same fish whose carcasses I had seen with PJ Bestelink — rampage up the channels in a noisy pre-breeding feast.

I witnessed the run at Guma Lagoon, a permanent body of water near the Panhandle. I heard it before I saw it: a run of barbels woke me in the night. I thought it was a hippo sloshing through the reeds. The run continued into the daylight. I watched their sinuous bodies churn the water. They thwacked the papyrus stalks with their tails to flush prey fish out of hiding and gulped air from the surface with an explosive popping sound.

I was about to get into the water but my guide pointed out two crocodiles drifting nearby. I satisfied myself with just putting my head under. The catfish passed within inches of my mask: bull-headed, tapering to an eel-like tail.

At the other end of the delta, Maun broiled in temperatures

of 40 degrees. Hot winds sandblasted the town and the sky was white with dust. The tambourine symphony of cicadas was deafening. Maunites call October the suicide month. Even the wandering donkeys looked more weary of living than usual.

I had returned to the delta to see the flipside of the flood: the Okavango in ebb. The Thamalakane River, where I had witnessed the arrival of the new water three months earlier, was again bone dry. Flay Million's garden was bare soil, not a plant to be seen. No children played in the riverbed. Only a few dust devils whirled in the heat haze. Yet in the 1980s the Thamalakane flowed all year round, delivering water to the delta's ultimate outlet: the Boteti River.

Eighty kilometres southeast of Maun, at a camp called Meno a Kwena, the tooth of the crocodile, I climbed 30 metres down the Boteti's crumbling banks to its broad, cracked bed. It was like visiting Ezekiel's valley of dry bones. Strewn about were carcasses of zebra and wildebeest, their sun-blackened skin stretched tight over bone, jaws frozen in a last gasp. These animals, following a genetically imprinted map, came to this place expecting to drink, but found instead a dry riverbed. There is still water here, but it is underground, the legacy of floods past. Larger animals can dig for it, but with each floodless year the water table drops a little farther out of reach.

David Dugmore, who runs the camp, has made it a personal mission to provide water for at least some of the thirsty animals. He pumps groundwater to fill a small waterhole. But he can't afford to keep the pump running continuously, and his is only one small relief station in a vast arid landscape, so animals continue to die. Maintaining the supply line is also a problem, he told me, pointing to lion toothmarks in the black plastic pipe that runs from pump to pool. 'The lions are so desperate for water they bite into the pipe, working their way along until they reach the waterhole,' he said.

An hour's drive along sandy tracks brought us to another poignant sight: a pod of hippopotamuses stranded in a syrupy pond. There was no water for miles upriver or down, so the hippos were marooned. There was little grazing to be had in this place of thorn trees and sand, so it was with relief that we saw a Botswana Wildlife Service ranger drive up and unload half a dozen haybales, which he cut open and spread beside the pool. The hippos trotted out of the water and began to munch. Were it not for their daily handout they would starve.

I wondered how long it would take for this pool to go the way of the catfish graveyard I had seen with PJ. And what did it say about water movement through the delta that once-healthy rivers were drying up?

Drought conditions in southern Africa are predicted to worsen in coming years as the climate warms. Yet according to hydrologists and climate researchers, there is an underlying 18-year oscillation in rainfall patterns in the region, and an 80-year cycle of high and low flood volumes. In the early 2000s, when I was there, the delta was coming to the end of the 40-year low part of the flood cycle. Flood volumes are predicted to increase, peaking mid-century. If that prediction comes to pass, the Boteti will fill. Life will return.

When David Livingstone asked the baYei people to explain the phenomenon of the Okavango flood, they told him that every year a chief who lived to the north — Mazzekiva by name — killed a man and threw his body into the river, after which the water would flow.

Livingstone never investigated the claim, but a century and a half after he posed his question to the baYei, I stood on a bullet-pocked concrete bridge in the Angolan highlands and watched boys fishing in the headwaters of the Rio Cubango, one of the two main tributaries that feed the Okavango River. I wondered how many bodies — sacrifices not to water but to war — had been thrown into this river during Angola's 27-year civil war.

I was near the town of Sambo, in the verdant grazing country of the Bié Plateau. It was November, and the summer rains were starting. The landowner, Celestino Jolomba, pointed to two military vehicles lying rusting under a eucalyptus tree. They had belonged to Jonas Savimbi, he said. Savimbi was the head of the National Union for the Total Independence of Angola (UNITA), one faction in the bloodshed, and this area had seen UNITA's last stand.

Driving here, I had passed gangs of workmen daubing white and red paint on stones placed on the roadside to warn of land mines. Nine million mines are estimated to remain in Angola, reaping their gruesome harvest of limbs and lives. In this place of death, it was strange to think that the water flowing beneath me was bringing life to a distant delta. In a few weeks the flood would start to rise in the Panhandle. Relief would come to the Okavango's parched plains. The miracle would begin again.

Among
sharks

THEY WERE SLEEPING, OR resting, I'm not sure which, but immobile, suspended like grey ghosts in the caverns and amphitheatres of Aliwal Shoal, 5 kilometres off the South African beach town of Umkomaas. With the merest twitch of the tip of their tail they adjusted their position, slowly rising and falling as if in a trance, while around the craggy rock walls sea goldies, a vivid orange tropical fish, swirled like autumn leaves. A yellow trumpetfish, looking more like a swimming piccolo than a horn, lurked in the shadows of this bewitching place.

If there is a signature shark species of South Africa's east coast, it is this one: the spotted ragged-tooth shark, known in Australia as the grey nurse and in the Americas as the sand tiger. South African ragged-tooth sharks migrate between their pupping and feeding grounds in the cool waters of the southern cape and the tropical waters off the coast of Mozambique, where females gestate their young. Aliwal Shoal, a marine protected area 50 kilometres south of Durban, is one of their mating areas, and a stopping-off point on their migratory route.

As a result of the Agulhas Current's southward shift of tropical water, Aliwal has some of the southernmost hard-coral communities in the world. Its crevices, caves and overhangs, the fossilised remains of a dune system that formed some 80,000 years ago, offer shelter and habitat to a variety of tropical and subtropical species. But it is for its large winter/ spring aggregation of ragged-tooth sharks and, in summer, tiger sharks that Aliwal has become especially popular with divers.

It is a strange thing to see a motionless shark. Many of the better-known shark species, such as mako, hammerhead and great white, must keep moving to oxygenate their gills. Ragged-tooth sharks and some other species can pump water through their mouths and over their gills, and so avoid the necessity of constant motion. Ragged-tooths also possess the ability, unique among sharks, of gulping air from the surface to achieve almost neutral buoyancy, and thus to float in midwater.

The sheen of their olive skin dappled with dark brown blotches, the humped back and bevelled snout, the small, pale eyes with a black speck at the centre — the half-dozen resting ragged-tooths I saw gave me plenty of time to linger over these details, and to focus on the feature that gives the shark its name: an orthodontist's nightmare of a mouth.

Unlike most sharks, which keep their hardware concealed behind their fixed crescent frowns, 'raggies', as South Africans call them, look as if they're holding a mouthful of nails. And unlike the white shark's dagger-like teeth, specialised for slicing, the front teeth of a ragged-tooth shark are slender and pointed for grasping prey, typically fish, while the back teeth have rasplike surfaces for gripping and crushing. At the front of the jaw each tooth has as many as four replacements in various stages of deployment, opening out like blades of a Swiss army knife.

Baby ragged-tooth sharks put their teeth to swift and

deadly use. In one of the few known instances of intrauterine cannibalism, the dominant embryo within each of the female's two uteruses eats its siblings before hatching as a metre-long superpup. This life strategy must have had merit when the sharks were plentiful, but now, coupled with a low reproductive rate — breeding adults give birth only every two or three years — the elimination of additional pups has contributed to a perilously low population. The species is listed as critically endangered.

I returned to Aliwal at dusk with Mark Addison and his wife, Gail, who live in nearby Umkomaas. With the coming of evening, raggies rouse themselves from their daytime somnolence and begin to focus on food. Mark has found that they will readily accept a free handout from him.

We dropped beneath choppy seas and a strong current to an open sandy area. Mark stuffed two plastic drums of bonito into a crevice, then took out several fish and placed them on the sandy seabed, held in place by rocks. I watched as a dozen sharks sniffed out the fish. They swam in languid circles, their snouts swinging within inches of me, then away. Most were females, around 1.5 metres long. There were a couple of larger males.

They reminded me of dogs searching for a bone, but they didn't seem particularly skilful scavengers. Often they would swim past a fish and apparently not notice it. Sometimes they would detect the prey but seize the rock instead. Such mistakes usually cost them a tooth or two, left behind on the sand like chips of white china. The loss of an occasional tooth is of little consequence. In the course of its life, a ragged-tooth shark might produce as many as 25,000 teeth at a rate of 1000 a year. They have between 40 and 45 rows in the upper jaw and between 37 and 40 in the lower. They can afford to lose a few.

I sensed something behind me, and half turned to see a shark at my shoulder. With the same economy of effort they all displayed, she glided past less than half a metre away. I could see the lacy flutter of her gill openings, the zigzag muscle blocks flexing in her flanks. Resting my hand on her back, I felt the sandpapery roughness of her skin, the firm blades of the two dorsal fins, the flex of the tail scything through the water.

Other fish had been attracted by the bait. Several very large grey-and-white dappled potato bass hung back at the edge of visibility, making occasional sorties into the feeding zone. A metre-wide ribbontail ray made a dramatic entrance, ruffling its wings like the skirts of a flamenco dancer.

Mark started hand-feeding the sharks, and passed me a bonito so I could do the same. Two or three sharks swam by, ignoring my offering, so I thrust the fish more pointedly under the nose of the next in line, a female, and the shark mouthed it hesitantly, delicately, as if sampling it for taste. I could feel the teeth pierce and compress the fish as she pulled it gently from my hand. Then the mouth opened and the fish was gone.

It all seemed very genteel, and very different from the melodramatic accounts I had read in childhood of heroic anglers battling this species of shark in northern Australia, where they were portrayed as ferocious man-eaters. The International Shark Attack File maintained by the Florida Museum — the most comprehensive database of shark–human interactions — ranks ragged-tooth sharks sixth in unprovoked attacks on humans, though there has never been a fatality attributed to a ragged-tooth shark. J. L. B. Smith, the doyen of South African fish scientists, believed ragged-tooths were 'a serious menace', and that the jaws of a large adult 'would easily sever a human head'. Was Smith uncritically parroting shark hyperbole, or are ragged-tooth sharks not always so mild-mannered as they are at Aliwal?

Mark believes ragged-tooth behaviour may be linked to water temperature. 'In the Cape, which is 10 to 15 degrees colder than Aliwal, raggies are much more aggressive,' he told me. 'Spear fishermen there talk of them with total respect and are very wary, whereas here we can spear fish in the midst of a bunch of raggies and not be hassled by them. But if the water temperature drops a few degrees, the gentle giant awakes. Their normally docile nature changes, and they become fish stealers.'

Sharks taking fish from humans is natural and unremarkable. Humans giving fish to sharks is controversial. People who are uneasy with the practice of feeding sharks argue that it threatens human safety. If sharks come to associate divers with food, they may mistake divers *for* food. Although there is no evidence of this, it is certainly true that sharks and other fish that are fed regularly by divers become 'diver positive', approaching their benefactors in expectation of a handout.

Another argument against feeding sharks is that supplementing the diet of any animal, terrestrial or aquatic, can be bad for the animal itself, either nutritionally or through fostering dependency on humans, or some other behavioural shift. 'Don't feed the wildlife' is a common injunction in locations where humans may be tempted to offer food to wild creatures. When I was reporting on the sardine run on the Wild Coast, signs in our accommodation informed us bluntly that to feed a monkey was to condemn it to death.

My grandfather, Leon Warne (left), was one of two skippers employed by Zane Grey to take him and his companion Laurie Mitchell fishing in 1926. Mitchell caught this 310-kilogram black marlin, and a few days later a 443-kilogram black marlin, a world record.

Leon, a boatbuilder as well as a game-fishing skipper, built his last launch, *Marline*, in 1949 in his boatshed at St Marys Bay, Auckland. *Marline* is owned today by my father, Kenneth (left). Dad remembers helping his father build the launch when he was in his late teens.

At two, I was already keen on the seashore. At 10, I had learned to carry a dinghy the way my father did, turtle fashion. Today, I spend summer holidays cruising on *Marline* in the Bay of Islands.

I dived with a hawksbill turtle at D'Arros Island during a *National Geographic* assignment on island conservation in the Seychelles. In Oman, for an assignment on Arabian seas, I joined volunteer reef guardians to cut snagged nets from coral.

National Geographic photographer David Doubilet, with whom I worked on three assignments, photographs a juvenile crocodile in the Okavango Delta. During my fieldwork I drank from the headwaters of the Okavango River in Angola.

Dive guide Mark Addison swims with a tiger shark at Aliwal Shoal during one of my South Africa assignments. A copper shark or bronze whaler cruises through a sardine shoal during the annual sardine migration along the Wild Coast of KwaZulu-Natal.

I reported on the threats to the coral reefs of the Philippines from overfishing and coral bleaching and visited Kiribati, where breaches in the seawalls illustrate the perils of rising sea levels to atoll communities.

On an assignment to the Gulf of St Lawrence's Magdalen Islands, I reported on the controversial hunting of harp seal pups. In Greenland, hunters see marine mammals as a gift of Sassuma Arnaa, the mother of the sea, here depicted in granite on the foreshore of the capital, Nuuk.

For marine creatures, the situation is less clear. It is well established that seabirds feeding on the discards from fishing vessels gain a valuable boost to their breeding chances. The fish scraps they are scavenging are the same type of food they would be foraging for themselves, so there is no issue about the quality of the nutrition — unlike, say, the feeding of deep-fried fish and chips to seagulls.

But the very fishing activities that provide high-value food scraps for seabirds are, in fact, likely to kill them. Seabird deaths through coming into contact with commercial fisheries run to hundreds of thousands per year and are the main reason why many albatross, petrel and other seabird species are now endangered. Seabird scientists have concluded that the harms from fisheries far outweigh their benefits, and best practice on fishing vessels now includes a zero discard policy, along with many other mitigation measures to keep seabirds safe.

For Aliwal's ragged-tooth sharks, perhaps the balance of benefit and harm from hand-feeding an occasional bonito is different. There is no suggestion that their migratory movements are being disrupted — the sharks are at Aliwal only temporarily, pausing here as part of an annual circuit. Would a free meal here create a permanent association in the shark's mind between divers and food? And given the catastrophic decline in all shark species through human exploitation of sharks for fins and meat, along with competition for diminishing fish stocks, would a little consideration in the other direction go astray?

One thing that is clear is that diver interactions with sharks seem to change the diver, if not the shark. I met and dived with several tourist divers at Aliwal who said they found the encounters enriching, an experience with wild nature to be treasured. I saw that response in Gail's eyes after our dusk dive. Eyes shining, she said, 'You must know how special this is.'

The feeding of ragged-tooths at Aliwal seemed to me an encounter where the sharks were not demeaned or paraded for human amusement. Divers are in the sharks' environment. Sharks can choose to interact or not, and they seem willing to do so. Mark said that over the years he's been diving with raggies at Aliwal they have become more curious and confident. They often swim between the legs of divers, perhaps enjoying the brush of sharkskin against wetsuit. And they seem to enjoy having their bellies scratched.

Mark helped pioneer shark diving on the KwaZulu-Natal coast, and believes that the more people who experience sharks face to face, the greater the chance of improving the conservation status of these maligned animals. The hope is that people might come with fear and leave with admiration; that prejudice might turn to praise.

I met a diver at Aliwal who used to loathe sharks. *Jaws* petrified her. She hyperventilated in the shark tunnel at Florida's SeaWorld. Now she is a born-again sharkophile. She and her husband take dive holidays in places where sharks can be encountered — and nowhere can sharks be more reliably encountered than in South Africa.

To dive with sharks is to begin to see them as they are, and not as we have represented them to ourselves. It is the beginning of a relationship reset. But in the case of great white shark tourism, the presumption of fear is integral to the product, and I'm not sure it is even possible to see these animals apart from their culturally defined stereotype of terror.

As part of my fieldwork for *National Geographic*, I visited Gansbaai (Afrikaans for Goose Bay) on the Western Cape, a two-hour drive from Cape Town, and one of South Africa's white shark tourism hubs. (South Africans drop the 'great' from the shark's name, perhaps because it's self-evident.)

Gansbaai straddles a peninsula. On one side is the town's fishing port, a drab assemblage of fish factories, boatyards and wharves, overlooked by a tall-spired church and picturesque pink, green and yellow painted houses. On the other side is Kleinbaai (Small Bay), which could justifiably rename itself Carchariasville, given the millions of rands that *Carcharodon carcharias* injects into the local economy. Among the souvenirs for sale in a stall beside the slipway were white shark T-shirts and beanies and bottles of port etched with a shark motif.

Shark-watching boats operate from Kleinbaai year round, though the winter months of May to September are the high season. The boats converge on a narrow channel between Dyer Island, a bird sanctuary, and Geyser Rock, a rookery for some 60,000 fur seals, the shark's chief prey. The channel has become known as Shark Alley. I was in a boat named *Swallow*, which struck me as having an unfortunate double meaning where sharks are concerned.

A deckhand ladled chum made from shark liver and tuna heads over the stern, creating a smelly slick on the water, and let out a seal-shaped decoy cut from thick black neoprene on a rope. A lingo has developed around this work. The decoy is a 'cookie', or 'koekie' in Afrikaans. 'Shark on the koekie! Shark on the koekie!' the deckhand shouts when a shark shows an interest. The decoy is hauled back to the boat in the hope that the shark will follow. A tuna head attached to a thick length of mooring hawser is thrown over the side to maintain the shark's interest. On *Swallow,* skipper Michael Rutzen also tossed overboard a cheesecloth bag of chopped frozen shark liver, known in the trade as a 'chumsicle'.

Once the shark is beside the boat, an orchestrated interaction ensues. 'Let the games begin,' said Rutzen, stepping onto a platform at the stern. Gansbaai's shark wranglers have found that they can lift a white shark's head out of the water and display its weaponry by reaching over the head to grasp the acutely sensitive snout. The animal opens its mouth repeatedly, as if trying to eat the air.

Scientists believe there is so much sensory apparatus in the snout of a white shark that the touch of a human hand leads to a state known as tonic immobility, a kind of suspended animation. It was remarkable to see an animal so culturally identified with aggression apparently mesmerised, gaping while a dozen cameras clicked, seawater pouring into the fleshy pink recesses of its mouth.

It was a stunning coup de théâtre. The sight of the most infamous teeth in the ocean — those gleaming triangles of death — guarantees gasps of awe from watchers. But I felt this handling of the shark crossed a line, turning a wildlife interaction into a circus performance.

According to biologists, the head of a shark is so packed with electroreceptors and olfactory organs that a shark can detect fish extracts at a concentration of less than one part in 10 billion, and will follow an odour corridor for kilometres to reach a dead or injured animal. Sharks can detect electricity at such low levels that if you were to dip one terminal of a car battery into the sea at the northernmost tip of the North Island and the other terminal at the southernmost point of the South Island, a shark could sense that electric field. Such a remarkable sensitivity should not be toyed with to produce a spectacle.

After viewing the sharks from the boat came the opportunity to view them underwater. The air was rich with the stench of the nearby seal colony, and the leafy tips of sea bamboo lifted and flopped at the surface like floor mops. I stepped into a cage that tilted and lurched with the lazy groundswell, and took an air regulator into my mouth as the cage was lowered. Visibility was poor, but through the murky water I could make out white sharks keeping their distance. I breathed slowly, as instructed, so as not to scare them with bubbles. 'Not to scare them' seems an ironic thing to say about an apex predator.

I went through the cage exercise because I believed my reporting for *National Geographic* required it, not because I wanted that sort of staged, controlled encounter. I would have preferred a free dive, but the poor visibility under water ruled out that option. No one who dives with white sharks wants to be a victim of mistaken identity.

Shark-diving enterprises like those at Gansbaai purport to raise awareness of the predicament of sharks — their global decline through overfishing. Perhaps they achieve this goal, but I came away thinking that shark education is a sideline to the central business of playing on people's fear. Sharks in these contexts are actors in an anthropocentric drama, not much different from 'Bruce', the mechanical shark that stood in for the real thing in *Jaws*.

But there's another aspect to this. At Gansbaai and other places where shark tourism has flourished, former fishers have become skippers of shark-watching and shark-diving boats. Instead of harvesting the seas in competition with marine predators, they take people to meet those predators. Does it come down to a choice: exploit fish as a food commodity or exploit sharks as an entertainment commodity?

For many people, the question distils to a simple logic: a live shark is better than a dead shark. As a shark poster I saw put it: 'Look at me a hundred times or kill me once.' And the world is awash in dead sharks. In 2012, Canadian researchers compiled data on global shark catches, reported and unreported, legal and illegal, and came up with the startling number of 100 million sharks killed each year. There is no reason to think that the number has declined since. The researchers warned that if such rates of shark killing continue, already stressed populations are unlikely to recover.

A quarter of the world's 470 shark species are threatened with extinction, among them the whale shark — the largest fish in the sea and the largest vertebrate on earth that is not a mammal. Longer than a city bus, gorgeously patterned like an Aboriginal dot painting, these placid, plankton-eating nomads ply the tropical oceans, from shallow coastal waters to depths of up to 2 kilometres.

Like whales, they have become tourist magnets, nowhere more so than at Oslob, near the southern tip of Cebu Island in the Philippines — the most popular whale shark-watching destination in the world. I visited the former fishing village while reporting on Philippines coral reefs for *National Geographic* in 2016. What surprised me was that most visitors didn't seem especially interested in the sharks themselves. What they wanted was a whale shark selfie: a 'me with the biggest fish in the world' picture to post on social media.

It was a strange sight: dozens of tourists in the water holding on to the outriggers of their whale-watching boats. Their backs were to the sharks while they mugged for the cellphones being clicked by the boat skippers. The heroes in the interaction were the humans; the beasts were the backdrop. It was shark posing more than shark watching. But this, evidently, is what people want. In 2018, half a million tourists came to pose with Oslob's whale sharks, spending NZ$15 million on tickets alone.

The operation is controversial, because Oslob, unlike other whale shark tourism sites in the Philippines and elsewhere in the world, is not a place where whale sharks congregate naturally. The Oslob sharks are here because they are fed, and it is this feeding that all but guarantees they will show up, day after day.

Whale sharks are plankton eaters. They spend between eight and twelve hours a day cruising the ocean with their mouths open, ingesting whatever planktonic life and small fish get in the way. They take in 600 cubic metres of water (a quarter of an Olympic swimming pool) an hour. It is not surprising that they have become regulars at the Oslob breakfast bar, where shrimp is always on offer.

But what effect does the feeding, not to mention the mingling with hundreds of humans on a daily basis, have on the animals' behaviour, socialisation and survival? As Oslob's popularity has grown, researchers have scrambled to try to answer these questions and to weigh the costs and benefits to the animals that are the star attraction.

Scientists with the Philippines' Large Marine Vertebrates Research Institute have studied the population structure and residency patterns of the Oslob sharks, analysed their feeding methods and tracked their movements by satellite. But even basic questions such as whether feeding them influences the seasonal migration of whale sharks remain unanswered.

Oslob's buffet begins at six in the morning, when the first tourist arrivals listen to a short briefing — no touching, no riding, no flash photography, keep at least 2 metres away from the sharks at all times — are kitted up with masks, snorkels and lifejackets and board outrigger boats to see the sharks. In the 'interaction area', 50 metres from shore, the boats line up and the show begins.

On the day I was at Oslob, 25 boats arranged themselves in a square. Feeders in small one-person outrigger canoes positioned themselves inside the square and started dishing out handfuls of thawed shrimp to the waiting sharks, many of which had timed their arrival to the site to within a few minutes of the start of feeding.

Visitors are warned they can go to jail if they touch or get too close to the sharks, but researchers have found that more than 95 per cent of swimmers break the rules, often inadvertently. It's a mêlée out there, a forest of legs in the water, with feeders flicking shrimp close to the tourist boats to draw the sharks in.

The sharks themselves are intent on the food, not the throng of humans splashing and jostling for the optimum image. Some swim languidly at a 45-degree angle to the surface. Others suspend themselves vertically as though their tails are weighted, slurping the shrimp with muscular gulps that suck a whirlpool of water and food into their postbox-slot mouths.

Feeding ceases at midday. The sharks dissipate and the boatmen disperse. Show's over, until tomorrow.

I talked to some of the boatmen about how Oslob had changed in the 10 years since shark-viewing tourism began, and how their lives had changed. The most obvious change has been economic. At night, the Oslob coastline twinkles with the lights of more than 50 hostels, resorts and guesthouses, as well as local residences. 'The whale sharks brought the lights,' one resident told me.

A reduction in fishing pressure around Oslob is another likely benefit. The 170 or so members of the local fishermen's association, who feed the sharks, ferry the guests and take the photos, no longer need to fish for food from increasingly impoverished reefs. Likewise, fishers from other locations, who now earn their living supplying the several hundred kilograms of shrimp needed for each day's shark provisioning, are placing less pressure on declining fish stocks or damaging coral reefs through destructive fishing techniques such as dynamiting.

Sixty per cent of the tourism revenue goes to the fishers, Mark Rendon, a 26-year-old boatman, told me. Thirty per cent goes to the municipality and 10 per cent to the local village.

Rendon has been part of the Oslob operation for three years. He used to work away from home in Cebu City as a government clerk. Now he earns more, travels less, has fewer expenses and lives at home with his family.

It is not only the boatmen who have benefited. 'Housewives have become entrepreneurs,' Rendon said, pointing to a row of stalls where women were peeling mangoes, making smoothies and selling sunglasses, T-shirts and crafts.

I asked him if he thought the sharks were being manipulated into staying at Oslob when they would normally just be passing through. 'The national aquarium has manta rays in tanks,' he replied. 'Our whale sharks can come or go as they please. We give them breakfast. They have to get their own lunch and dinner.'

That's true. Most whale sharks visit Oslob for a few days

or weeks and move on, though some (4 per cent of the total) become year-round residents. Some scientists worry that sharks that take advantage of the free feed for prolonged periods may suffer ill effects, both physiologically and behaviourally. The shrimp they're fed is a less diverse mix of planktonic creatures than what they would consume naturally. It's not junk food, but neither is it necessarily a healthy diet.

Another concern is that once sharks associate boats with free food at Oslob, that connection could lead them into danger elsewhere. Almost half of the whale sharks that have been studied at Oslob have propeller cuts on their bodies. These come not from the operation itself, where all vessels are hand-paddled, but from motorised boats elsewhere.

A more deadly hazard exists. A young whale shark habituated to boats might one day approach a shark-fishing vessel. Whale sharks have been nationally protected in the Philippines since 1998, but they range widely across the ocean, including into waters where they may not have legal protection. And even in the Philippines, poaching persists.

When migratory animals are conditioned to remain in one place for an extended period of time, what effect does this have on their usual patterns of interaction — with other members of their species, with potential mates, with seasonal food sources? Research is yet to provide answers to those questions. But what is known is that of the 650 individual whale sharks that have been identified in the Philippines, a quarter have been seen at Oslob. That's a significant portion of the population being exposed to unknown survival risks.

Some argue that whale sharks, like whales, pandas, polar bears, tigers and elephants, have become ambassadors for the natural world — charismatic creatures that move people to care for the planet — and that a degree of disturbance through the provision of food and the presence of humans in their midst is offset by a wider conservation consciousness and a growing esteem for the creatures of the sea.

It would be nice to think that for every tourist giving a thumbs-up to the cellphone camera while a shark swims obligingly past, there is another who looks into the eye of that great spotted giant and sees something of immense intrinsic worth, whose existence must be protected and whose world conserved.

But this may be wishful thinking. A recent scientific study of how tourists perceive the Oslob whale shark operation found that many visitors are aware that feeding an endangered species for tourism purposes is ethically problematic, but take part anyway. A 'guilty pleasure' is how they rationalise the experience.

The boatmen I met feared the government might decide the conservation risks outweighed the economic benefits and ban the feeding of sharks, which would, in effect, end the operation. They hoped that wouldn't happen — that the educational component of the experience would be seen to offset the ecological impacts. And in a country such as the Philippines, where many fishing households are at poverty level, who would gainsay the windfall that has come to Oslob by something as simple as throwing handfuls of shrimp into the mouths of passing sharks?

Attitudes are changing, and they need to continue to change if sharks are to have a secure future. When I was a university student in the 1970s fear of sharks was endemic and largely unquestioned. I recall a collecting trip to the Three Kings Islands when I was beginning the fieldwork for my master's degree in classifying sponges. I was aboard a Ministry of Agriculture and Fisheries research vessel. At dusk one evening I was snorkelling some distance from the vessel when a crewman rowed rapidly towards me and called in an urgent voice, 'Get into the dinghy! There's a bronze whaler around.' I didn't hesitate, launching myself over the gunwale, fins flailing.

How different from 25 years later, when the sight of bronze whalers spiralling up from the blue depths of the Indian Ocean or plunging into sardine baitballs on South Africa's Wild Coast would hold me transfixed. Or from recent summers in the Bay of Islands, where sharks of the same species are starting to come into bays where I have never seen them before.

Those early fears strike me today as archaic, on a par with the dread and horror people once harboured towards octopuses. Those supremely intelligent molluscs are now an inspiration, as evidenced in the popular documentary *My Octopus Teacher*, filmed in the same kelp forests I wrote about in my South Africa stories for *National Geographic*.

But even the great sea champion Jacques Cousteau was not immune to shark loathing. His treatment of sharks in *The Silent World* is disconcerting, to say the least. Midway through the movie, Cousteau's ship, the legendary *Calypso*, chasing a pod of sperm whales in the Indian Ocean, collides with a young whale. Billows of blood drift from the lacerated whale and attract a bevy of sharks — the 'mortal enemies' of divers, intones Cousteau.

'We have met them before, but never so many and none so hungry,' he adds as *Calypso*'s 'anti-shark' cage is lowered into the water with the fearless filmmakers inside. Cousteau's voiceover ratchets up the drama. 'This underwater dance of death has never been seen by any man who lived to tell the tale,' he says, his words given additional heft by a tension-building orchestral score. 'A dead whale or a man in the sea — it's the same thing to sharks. Then comes the first bite. It is the signal for the orgy to begin.'

But whose orgy? After dwelling on the feeding sharks, the camera shifts to the decks of *Calypso*, where sharks are being dragged aboard with hooks and gaffs and bludgeoned to death with sledgehammers, to 'avenge the whale'. I couldn't believe my eyes. This from the underwater Attenborough!

No nature documentary would use such footage today. But the fear-and-loathing legacy clings like a suckerfish, and needs to be tackled at its root: the loss of connection between humans and nature that pervades the Western tradition. Instead of a yin–yang complementarity, we have inherited — and perpetuated — a yes–no separation, or at the very least a perplexing ambivalence: the tension of being both part of, and apart from, the natural world. 'Both in and out of the game and watching and wondering at it', as Walt Whitman put it.

Stuck in our categorical boxes of human/non-human, we lack the vocabulary and modes of discourse that many traditional societies still retain — their effortless conversation with non-human nature, including with sharks. It's a nuanced and complex relationship. There is nothing soft or sentimental about it. Sharks are ancestors, sharks are food for humans and humans are occasionally food for sharks.

In Hawaiian culture, sharks are highly respected, and kahu or shark keepers consult specific 'aumakua —ancestors whose spirits are embodied as shark guardians and protectors. In Papua New Guinea, where sharks are hunted for food, shark callers paddle out to the deep and chant: 'Sun come up, my shark come up.' When sharks appear they are lured to the boat with rattles and songs, then noosed and wrestled aboard. The community feasts on the catch.

Towards the end of *The Silent World* is a lengthy segment shot at Aldabra, the westernmost fleck of land in the Seychelles, 800 kilometres from the African coast. It was there in 2015, in water not much more than ankle deep, that I floated among Cousteau's 'mortal enemies', 20 or more blacktip reef sharks. They come to the beach in front of the research station every high tide, languidly cruising the shallows as the sea ebbs, until their dorsal fins are fully clear of the water and their bellies scrape the sand.

Pale skin against the pale sand, they passed like wraiths with jet-black fin tips and large, attentive eyes, circling the man with a mask in their midst. I was there, they were there. That was all. Human and non-human, in the dance of life.

Under
the ice

I AM FLOATING IN A netherworld of billowing green ice clouds and shadowy canyons, the winter kingdom of Canada's Gulf of St Lawrence. Shafts of light lance the surface waters but are quenched by the serge-grey depths. Translucent comb jellies drift past, slaves to the current. I keep out of their way. If I come into contact with their fragile bodies they will break into smeary cytoplasmic strands.

Photographer Brian Skerry glides by with one of his camera rigs. The contraption, with its glass Cyclops eye, jointed legs and flashlight feet, looks suitably extraterrestrial for this alien environment. We swim awkwardly in our icewater dive gear: a Kevlar drysuit, layers of polypropylene next to our skin, thick rubber gloves, a neoprene hood. Brian has an electric chest-warmer powered by a battery clipped to his weight belt. My temperature gauge reads −2°C.

We are waiting for harp seals to appear, hoping that some will be curious about these bulky terrestrials who have entered their domain. On the ice a stealthy approach can bring us to within a metre of the animals, but underwater encounters are at their discretion. Usually they keep their distance, and we glimpse them only as ghostly torpedoes on the edge of visibility.

Today the seals draw a little nearer, inspecting us with bulging eyes. One twists upside down, revealing the harp-shaped blotch on its back that gives these seals their name.

Their hind flippers splay and fold like Japanese fans, propelling the animals with graceful, powerful strokes. On the ice, it is the fore flippers that provide propulsion. Equipped with claw crampons, the 130-kilogram animals heave themselves along, while their folded hind flippers swish from side to side like a whisk broom. This tobogganing gait only works on smooth ice; on rough, hummocky ice the animals hump and wriggle like overweight caterpillars.

The seals' curiosity doesn't last long. After only a few minutes they recede into the dark depths, where I have neither the speed nor the air to follow them. Harp seals can dive to 250 metres and swim at 30 kilometres an hour.

I surface in a gap between floes and grasp the edge of the ice. It disintegrates into a thistledown of spicules that prick my lips, the only exposed part of my body. Nearby, female harp seals bob in the margarita slush, peering over the lip of ice to check on their pups.

It was mid-March, 2003, and I was in the Magdalen Islands to witness the southern sojourn of *Pagophilus groenlandicus*, 'the ice-lover from Greenland', and write about the experience for *National Geographic*. March is the high season for harp seals. They have migrated 3000 kilometres from Baffin Bay and the northern coasts of Greenland to reach their traditional spring quarters in the Gulf of St Lawrence and on the coasts of Labrador and Newfoundland. All the big events of their lives — mating, giving birth, moulting —

happen here, where blizzards rake the frozen sea and currents crumple the floes into an icy Stonehenge.

The timing of the assignment was significant. Forty years earlier, a bitter controversy had broken out between Canadian sealers and animal welfare groups over the hunting of baby harp seals. The harp seal pup, with its fluffy white coat and black pleading eyes, became the darling of the anti-fur movement and a symbol of all that was wrong with human exploitation of nature.

After nearly two decades of fervent protest, the European Economic Community bowed to pressure from environmentalists and in 1983 banned the importation of whitecoat pelts and all harp seal products, a mandate that crippled the Canadian seal trade. For many the battle ended there: a victory for nature. But fur was coming back into fashion, and although the whitecoat pup remained protected under Canadian law, the hunt for older pups was booming. More harp seals were taken in the early 2000s than at any other time in the previous 35 years. The North Atlantic seal hunt had become the largest marine mammal hunt in the world.

Given this renewed pressure, I wanted to find out how the species was faring. Had protest and legislation secured the harp seal's future? Or was *Pagophilus* destined to go the way of the walruses and great whales, its surviving populations only pathetic remnants of a once great horde?

When I arrived, the Magdalen Islands, an archipelago in the shape of a fishhook midway between Prince Edward Island and Newfoundland, lay clenched in the fist of winter and shivered in sub-zero temperatures. To reach the harp seal pupping grounds required a 50-kilometre helicopter flight from the islands across the sea ice. Typically, we could make this trip one day in three.

Fog, snow flurries or freezing rain kept the machines on the ground for the other two. I could see them from my motel room: two frozen dragonflies waiting for the sun.

When we did fly, it was like an introductory lesson in the myriad manifestations of ice. Sheets of newly frozen ice looked like overlapping panes of frosted glass. There were floes the size of pancakes, lily pads, hockey rinks. At one moment we seemed to be flying over the mother of all wedding cakes; at another, it looked as if someone had taken a sledgehammer to the place, and a billion bits of berg were drifting in a blue-black sea.

Our eyes strained to pick out the whelping patches: clusters of harp seal mothers and pups resting beside leads of open water. Frozen afterbirth and smudges of blood on the ice showed where pups had been born. Seal trails crisscrossed the snow like snail trails through frost.

Sea ice is critical to harp seals for giving birth and nursing pups and, several weeks later, for moulting. The ice has to be thick and stable enough to support the seals, but not so thick that they cannot make and maintain their breathing holes.

But sea ice is highly variable, subject to the caprices of wind, current and air temperature. Some years it breaks up early, plunging pups into the sea before they have enough blubber to withstand the cold. Other years it lingers late into spring and is jammed and crumpled against the coast. Pups, unable to reach open water, are crushed between its grinding slabs.

A light ice year can result in catastrophic mortality. In 1981, almost every pup born in the gulf died due to early break-up of ice. On average, such disasters occur every 10 years or so, say harp seal scientists. But if global warming were to increase the occurrence to once in every five years, or three, the population would be in trouble.

Clearly there was no problem with the ice this year, I thought, as I stumped across the wind-sculpted ice prairies of a whelping patch. The yowling, mewing, gargling and wailing of pups filled the air. Some scuffled their way across the ice, pushing up little bow waves of snow with their puppy-like snouts. Others nestled in ice cradles formed by their own body heat.

Many were spectacularly fat. They lay on the ice like portly powder puffs, their heads pulled into their shoulders, fur fluffed up, eyes half closed and moist with tears. (Lacking the tiny ducts that remove excess tears, their eyes weep constantly.) After a couple of weeks their silky white foetal hair — the lanugo — starts falling out, revealing a dappled grey coat beneath.

Stacking on fat is vital for these young pups. Although they can swim almost from birth, they need the thermal insulation of a thick blubber layer to survive in frigid seas. So during the first days of their lives they gorge themselves on one of the richest milks in all of nature — 12 times more fatty and 25 times richer in protein than cow's milk — putting on up to 3 kilograms a day. At weaning — around 10 to 12 days old — they weigh more than 30 kilos. Blubber is so important for survival that weaned harp seals burn protein for their metabolism, rather than their insulating blubber layer, while they learn to hunt at sea.

The white fur of the pups is so thick and fluffy that young ones struggle to get under the water. They dog-paddle through the slush ice, which bulges over their backs as they swim, until eventually their pelage loses enough air for them to dive.

To the European settlers of the region, harp seals must have looked like fur-coated barrels of lard, abundant and free for the taking. And take them they did. By the 1850s more than half a million harp seals — most of them whitecoat pups — were being killed during the annual hunting season. Oil, not fur, was the primary product. The seal oil of Newfoundland lubricated the sewing machines of England.

The fur itself did not become popular until the late 1940s. Before then there was no technology to keep the luxuriant white lanugo from falling out of the dressed skin, so seal pelts were instead tanned into leather. After 1945, however, Norwegian advances in fur dressing meant that the harp seal pelt could be marketed as a fur. Demand rose quickly, at a time when harp seal populations were already in decline. By 1972 the Newfoundland–Gulf of St Lawrence harp seal stock stood at less than 2 million animals. In 1976, as debate over the hunt was heating up, seal scientist David Lavigne warned in a cover story for *National Geographic* that 'the survival of the harp seal hangs in the balance'.

His warning would become a call to arms. Two centuries after Moravian missionaries in Labrador chose the harp seal pup to explain the Lamb of God to the Inuit (who had never seen a sheep), environmental crusaders, alarmed by the seal's declining numbers and outraged that hunters were targeting pups not yet weaned from their mother's milk, vowed to stop the slaughter of the innocents.

Car licence plates in Quebec — which includes the Magdalen Islands, or Îles de la Madeleine — bear the legend 'Je me souviens', 'I remember'. The Madelinots, as the 95 per cent of islanders who are French-speaking call themselves, do not easily let go of their 250 years of history

and traditions. They remember the dark days following
1755 when, fleeing deportation by the British, the islands'
founding families made their way there from what is now
Nova Scotia to start a new life. Originally farming folk, these
exiled Acadians were forced to turn to the sea for sustenance.
La mer became la mère, and for many of them the sea is still
a mother. A thousand of the 13,000 islanders fish for a living,
and a similar number process the catches of lobster, crab,
herring and mackerel.

Madelinot fishers also remember the two decades of
tribulation that began in the 1960s when anti-hunt campaigners,
spearheaded by the International Fund for Animal Welfare and
later by Greenpeace, triggered the eventual collapse of the seal
trade. Portrayed as murderers and barbarians, fishers suffered
the contempt of the masses as television brought graphic scenes
from the icefields of the North Atlantic into the living rooms of
Europe and North America. A Greenpeace billboard showed a
fashionable woman in short skirt and high heels trailing a blood-
drenched fur coat. 'It takes up to 40 dumb animals to make a fur
coat,' ran the text, 'But only one to wear it.'

Taking part in what had been known as the greatest hunt
in the world — an enterprise that in the nineteenth century
had involved more than 13,000 men and 400 sailing ships —
was no longer a matter of pride but a mark of shame. Once
hailed as 'Vikings of the ice', the sealers were now the scum
of the earth. The Madelinots' cries of 'Nous ne sommes pas
des bouchers!' — 'We are not butchers!' — sounded hollow
when accompanied by photographs of upraised clubs and
bloodstained ice, or of Brigitte Bardot cuddling a baby seal.

Jocelyn Thériault was a youngster when the protests peaked.
When I met him he was 33 and owned a one-third share in

a 20-metre fishing boat, *Manon Yvon*. He, his brother and a cousin fished for snow crab and redfish. They used to fish for cod, too, but in April 2003 the North Atlantic cod fishery, which had failed to recover despite closures and dramatically reduced harvests, was shut down indefinitely by the Canadian government. The stock remains precariously low to this day.

The demise of the cod industry gave renewed impetus to modern-day harp seal hunters. The livelihood of fishers like Jocelyn depends on harvesting whatever the sea has to offer — including seals. Since 1987, when Canada outlawed commercial hunting of whitecoat pups, the main focus of the hunt has been moulted pups, known as beaters — so named because they tend to thrash the water when they swim, not because the traditional method of killing them is with clubs. In 2003, beater pelts were worth the equivalent of NZ$50 to a hunter.

I met Jocelyn at the wharf in Cap aux Meules, the commercial centre of the islands. He and his crew were loading supplies for the seal hunt, set to begin in a couple of days, ice permitting. I walked a slippery plank from the dock to the deck of *Manon Yvon*, stamped the snow off my boots and climbed a ladder to the wheelhouse, where Jocelyn was poring over printouts of the latest ice maps on his chart table.

Like all fishers in this region of ice-bound winter coasts, he can work only eight months of the year. For the remainder he is on an unemployment benefit. With a 1.5-million-dollar boat to pay off, four months is a long time without significant income — and a long time to be ashore if your life is the sea.

Jocelyn has been seal hunting for eight years. In a good year — navigable ice, accessible seals, firm prices for pelts and oil — he and his crew of 12 can jointly earn $150,000 during the spring hunt. But like other fishers, he derives only about

5 per cent of his earnings from harp seals. It doesn't sound worth the effort until you consider the other reason fishers hunt seals: they argue that the animals compete for the very thing that puts food on the family table. In French, the harp seal is loup-marin de glace, sea wolf of the ice.

Biologists estimate that an adult harp seal consumes more than a tonne of fish a year — mostly capelin, sand lance and arctic cod — along with invertebrates such as crabs, shrimp and krill. Cumulatively, harp seals are thought to account for more than 80 per cent of the estimated 4 million tonnes of fish and zooplankton consumed by all seal species in the Northwest Atlantic. In the fishers' arithmetic, that equates to a lot of seafood not going into their nets. Cull the harp seal population, they say, and you level the playing field.

Critics scoff at this logic: they accuse the fishers of wanting the whole field to themselves. Given the myriad interactions between marine organisms, it is folly to suppose that culling one species will increase the population of another. Opponents accuse fishers of wanting to play God with the resources of the sea. While the history of overexploited fisheries more than backs up this view, fishers say they have learned from past mistakes. 'I am a new generation of fisher,' Jocelyn insisted. 'I don't want to kill all the seals, just make a fair play.'

What constitutes fair play is ultimately a political decision. Out on the ice floes I met Mike Hammill, a seal biologist whose work helps the Canadian government manage its marine resources.

'You picked a nice day for it,' he said as I stepped down from the helicopter, his frost-reddened face breaking into a grin. The temperature was −25°C and the wind stung like peroxide.

Around us it was business as usual in the harp seal nursery. Pups bawled like lost toddlers in a supermarket. Sleepy-eyed newborns nursed in utter contentment from mothers lying in Rubenesque repose. One mother languidly combed her pup's fur with her fore flipper as it suckled. Another, having finished nursing her infant, tried to go down a breathing hole that was too small for her, and became stuck, like Pooh Bear in Rabbit's front door, and had to gyrate furiously to get through.

Many pups lay in the lee of ice ridges, sheltered from the blasting wind. One was so fat it looked to have been inflated. I placed a gloved hand on the fur of its back — so thick, so soft. I lay next to another pup and watched tears forming in the glistening black globes of its eyes, run down its fur and drop onto the snow. It was these images of the crying bébé that sparked such outrage against the 'butchers of the Arctic'.

Along with whitecoat pups (which the Madelinots call blanchons) there were several 'ragged-jackets' — pups between 15 and 30 days old that were losing their baby fur. Some were nearing the end of the moult, the last of their white coats flaking off in swatches from the sleek grey fur beneath.

Here and there fully moulted beater pups lay like silver jellybeans on the ice. Their mottled pelage, which gradually turns khaki and brindled-black with successive moults, shimmered in many shades of grey, from metallic through pewter.

Pups at this stage have been recently abandoned by their mothers and must fend for themselves. For now, they have little to fear from predators: orcas, polar bears and Greenland sharks take harp seals in the Arctic, but don't follow them to their breeding grounds in the gulf.

For Mike, a senior scientist with Canada's Department of Fisheries and Oceans (DFO), this was a familiar scene. He has been studying the North Atlantic harp seal population for more than 30 years, working to produce a model of the harp seal population based on such factors as how many seals are born each year, how many die, and how many are in each age group. The model assists the government in setting a supremely important number: the total allowable catch (TAC). In the government's eyes, a fair TAC is one that maximises the sealers' returns without compromising the harp seal stock. Invariably, sealers consider it to be too low and conservationists too high.

I watched as Mike crept towards a resting female, carrying two long aluminium poles with a piece of fishing net stretched between. He broke into a run, threw the net, then dived onto the startled animal. An assistant helped him turn the seal over and tie the ends of the poles together. Once pinned, the seal became as placid as her pup, watching from a few feet away.

Using a block and tackle mounted on a tripod, the researchers weighed both mother and pup, then measured and tagged them. After anesthetising the mother, Mike extracted a tooth. Counting the layers of dentine is the most efficient way of determining a harp seal's age.

This work was part of an annual live capture programme designed to help fine-tune the population model. By following the reproductive fortunes of a range of females of varying ages, Mike and his colleagues hoped to formulate a relationship between population density and reproductive rate, and also to find out what impact bad ice years have on the long-term fortunes of the seal herd.

Mike explained that the DFO's management objective for harp seals is a long-term sustainable harvest, using the TAC

— broken down into quotas for each sealing area — to control the population. It's the same approach New Zealand and several other countries use to manage fish stocks. In 2003, the department considered harp seals to be abundant, so had set a relatively generous TAC — 975,000 for the three years from 2003 to 2005. Hunters could take up to 350,000 seals during any two of those years, but the total for the three years could not exceed the TAC.

If the quotas were filled, it would drive the population down, but not too far down — that was the rationale. To guard against the possibility of a collapse, the DFO had established benchmarks at 70 per cent, 50 per cent and 30 per cent of 5.5 million, the highest estimate of the population in recent times.

'The government is committed to keeping the population above the 70 per cent benchmark of 3.85 million,' Mike explained. 'If it dips below that number, conservation measures such as lowering the TAC will follow. If the population hits the critical warning point — the 30 per cent benchmark, or 1.65 million — we will shut the hunt down.'

At that time, the harp seal was the second most abundant seal in the world, behind the crabeater seal of Antarctica. At 5.2 million, the population was at the level it was in the early 1970s. A pup census conducted in 1999 counted almost a million pups born that year.

In theory, given a healthy stock of long-lived adults (harp seals live for 30 years and start breeding between four and eight years old), juveniles can be hunted in relatively high numbers without jeopardising the population. But opponents of the hunt say the DFO's management approach is based on shaky assumptions. They accuse the government of taking unacceptable risks with a species that is directly threatened by a warming climate. If harp seals don't have sea ice, they can't breed and won't survive.

But that's overstating the problem. Even in a good ice year, at most a third of Northwest Atlantic harp seals bear their pups in the Gulf of St Lawrence. The majority give birth along the ice-bound shores of Labrador and western Newfoundland. In his latest assessment of the harp seal population in 2021, Mike noted that most of the gulf is predicted to be ice-free by the end of the century, but that this might not be the catastrophe that anti-sealing advocates claim. There will simply be a northward shift in distribution. 'They'll gradually disappear from the gulf, so instead of a third of harp seal pups being born there, maybe all the pups will be born off the Labrador coast,' he says.

By late March the days were warming, the islands thawing. It was the time of year the Madelinots call le reveil du printemps, the awakening of spring. Gobbets of ice fell from the powerlines and exploded in puffs of white on the tar roads. Diggers scooped ice away from boat ramps, and a mobile crane lifted craft that had been lying idle on blocks all winter back into the water. I lingered over their names: *Pelican, Sushi Provider, David's Last, Dickson's Dream.*

For fishers, this time of year is a release, a chance to feel salt wind on the face and the throb of the engine below deck. For the community, it is also a time of celebration. I was invited to celebrate Mi-Carême, mid-Lent, at the community of Fatima, when neighbours come together to enjoy Acadian music, a meal of duck and goose stew and an adult version of trick-or-treat, where people dress up in outrageous costumes and crazy masks and parade house to house for sweets and alcohol.

The festival is said to have originated as a break from Lenten self-denial, which struck me as a quintessentially French response to abstinence: balance it with a binge. I had my violin with me, and joined Acadian fiddler René Déraspe in some reels and hornpipes. It was a joyous evening. Outside the snow was thick on the ground, but inside the warmth of Madelinot hospitality banished winter's privations.

The following evening I joined fishing captain Denis Eloquin and his crew, bringing Denis's fishing boat *Jean-Mathieu* from Cap aux Meules to Grande Entrée. The sea was awash with broken ice floes, but *Jean-Mathieu*'s hull pushed them aside as if they were mahjong tiles. The orange beam of a searchlight lit the icefield ahead as Denis eased the boat through. I was on the foredeck, and looking back to the bridge I saw his face palely illuminated by the glow of the chart plotter and the sweeping green cursor of the radar. His hand rested on the steering control mounted beside his chair.

We went below for pork and seal casserole. The captain opened a bottle of vin rouge. I had the sense that the crew were checking me out, to see how the foreign journalist would react to being served seal. The meat was very dark red and gamey — not unpleasant, but nor was it a taste to make my mouth water. It could have been worse. In Newfoundland I might have been offered seal flipper pie, a traditional delicacy.

At Cap aux Meules, I noticed that *Manon Yvon*'s berth was empty. Jocelyn and his crew were out in the sea ice somewhere, ramming their way through the floes. But for smaller vessels the ice was still too thick. Most fishers would forgo their allotment of seals this year. One boat, *Frolic*, did risk the sea — and never returned. The crew were rescued, but the boat sank, another corpse for the 'graveyard of the gulf'.

Within two months, however, the gulf ice would have disappeared, flushed into the Atlantic. The harp seals would have gone too, their automatic pilots set to north for the 3000-kilometre journey back to the Arctic.

The coming and going of ice, seals and sealers has been happening for a long time. In the Magdalen Museum of the Sea, I came across a coin that evoked this tradition. It was a copper token, struck during the early 1800s and used briefly as currency in the islands. One side depicted a harp seal, the other a cod — two commercial staples of Magdalen life. The coin carried the motto, 'Success to the fishery' — a slogan that has become a mockery with the collapse of the commercial cod fishery. Few deny that it was driven into the ground by human greed.

Conversely, the seal hunt has endured. Catches in the 2000s approached levels of those a century earlier — between 200,000 and 300,000 a year, excluding the hundred thousand or so taken annually by Inuit sealers in Greenland. In 2002 the value of harp seal products landed in Canada exceeded Can$22 million, the highest in recent memory.

Most of the money is in the pelts, though there is still a multimillion-dollar market for harp seal oil. No longer used for sewing machines, the oil is now prized for its high content of omega-3 fatty acids. Processed into capsules, it is sold as a health supplement.

In the past 20 years catches have fallen, due not to a drop in harp seal numbers or a reduction in the TAC, but declining demand for fur. Between 2004 and 2019, harp seal catches declined by an order of magnitude, from more than 300,000 to around 30,000. In 2021 the total value of exported harp seal products from Canada was a paltry Can$200,000.

The harp seal population itself remains robust. At the most recent count, in 2017, there were an estimated 7.6 million harp seals off the east coast of Canada, up from 7.4 million in 2014. For 2022, the Canadian government set the TAC at 400,000.

Contrary to the claim that the seal hunt is endangering the species' future, the Northwest Atlantic harp seal population represents a conservation success story, says Mike Hammill. Numbers have increased from as low as 1.1 million animals in the early 1970s to over 7 million animals in the current decade, and that sevenfold increase occurred during a period of declining pregnancy rates. Mike attributes the population growth to reduced catches, limits on harvesting, a low frequency of poor ice years and an adaptive management approach that took these changes into account.

Yet an ideological battle still rages between those who view sealing as a legitimate use of a renewable resource and those who believe seals, along with whales and dolphins, should be above exploitation. For now the Canadian government has opted for sustainable use, a decision that distresses animal rights advocates but allows fishers like Jocelyn and Denis to maintain a way of life they cherish.

At the time I wrote the story I wasn't much impressed by the overblown rhetoric of the anti-sealing movement, which made exaggerated claims about the loss of sea ice leading to cataclysmic mortality in harp seal pups and a crisis for harp seal survival. My sympathy leaned toward the hunters, who I felt had been unfairly vilified.

I ended my *National Geographic* story with a question: 'Look at a harp seal and what do you see? Lamb of God or wolf of the sea? Nature's sanctity or nature's utility? Perhaps it is possible to see both.'

Inuit, who have been hunting seals longer than anyone, certainly have that view. For them there is no conflict between revering an animal and killing an animal. Indeed, there is no other way in which to take an animal. Hunting is sacred business.

In the West, there is little that is sacred in commercial hunting and fishing. A prevailing worldview of human dominion and a categorical separation between humans and nature has consistently led to attitudes of entitlement and practices of over-exploitation.

The Madelinot hunter-fishers struck me as lying somewhere between rapacious Western exploiters and subsistence indigenous harvesters. I saw humility in a small printed prayer Jocelyn Thériault had tacked above the window of the bridge on *Manon Yvon*, with a silver crucifix dangling from it. His grandmother gave him the note when he launched the boat. In translation, the prayer read: 'Lord, my vessel is small and your sea is vast. Help me this day, for the riches of the sea belong to you. Merci.'

These days in the islands, at the turning of the seasons, I found deeply appealing. I saw a house for sale, Maison Grenouille I believe it was called, named for a frog-filled pond on the property. I had a strong, completely impractical impulse to buy it. The land extended out to red-earth cliffs that had been pounded steep by the sea. The indigenous Mi'kmaq name for the islands, Menagoesenog, means 'battered by waves'. I could imagine writing in a hut on those cliffs, energised by the hammer blows of wind and sea.

One evening I drove to a frozen lagoon and took it into my head to walk on the ice. It was the novelty of it, I suppose — the thought of living somewhere where snow and ice are as familiar in winter as sun and sand are in summer. It was dusk, and the setting sun was flaming in the windows of the gingerbread houses that are such a feature of islands in the far north. As I walked towards a headland, the ice started to crack and split in front of my shoes. Nobody knew I was there, and I had visions of falling through, with possibly dire consequences. I tiptoed back to dry land, arms outstretched like a bird's wings to grab at the ice if it gave way.

What is it that affects a person about a particular combination of landscape and culture? I loved the islands' blend of French chic and seafarer salt. I loved driving a ribbon of asphalt in a snow-covered landscape. The history of the Acadians moved me, too, especially their own trail of tears after their expulsion by the British. Many travelled all the way to Louisiana, where their name, Acadiens, became Cajun.

On my last night in the islands, Bertrand Déraspe, the Magdalens' most acclaimed fiddler, came to the house where I was staying. We swapped a few tunes, then I put away my instrument and just listened, which is what you do in the presence of greatness. Bertrand would lean forward on his chair and say something like ''Ere is a tune I learned from a woodcutter' and start into some soulful melody that gradually increased in volume and speed until both his legs were pounding up and down on the wooden floor, beads of sweat standing out on his forehead and the musical equivalent of sparks flying from his bow.

Where I came to with the harp seal story was the thought that it is possible to balance needs and interests in the sea — seal welfare, island economy, cultural tradition. Never easy, but possible.

Grasping
the blade

O N MY LAST DAY in Manila, at the end of a month of diving and travelling around the Philippines for a *National Geographic* story on the future of coral reefs, I happened to pass a church dedicated to 'Our Lady of Remedies'. Given all that I had seen and learned in the previous weeks about the beleaguered state of coral reefs, it seemed appropriate to hope that a remedy, divine or otherwise, might appear for these ecosystems, which biologists warn will be functionally extinct by the end of the century, even by mid-century at the current rate of climate warming.

The disappearance of coral reefs takes some thinking about. It is said that if an extra-terrestrial surveyed our planet for signs of life, what they would see would be coral reefs. Coral reefs are the only evidence of life on earth that is visible from space. Could these stupendous structures, the glory of the oceans for 240 million years, really vanish?

On an ecological level, their loss would be an erasure of living things on an almost immeasurable scale. Although they occupy less than a quarter of 1 per cent of the marine environment, coral reefs are home to a quarter of all marine life. Their demise would also be an incalculable tragedy for human beings. Coral reefs provide sustenance and livelihoods for a billion people. Their colour-drenched beauty and vibrant diversity enchants millions more.

National Geographic wanted to report on the rising threat to reefs and let readers know that their future was in jeopardy. The natural location for such a story was the area of the Indo-Pacific known as the Coral Triangle, which includes the waters of Indonesia, Malaysia, Papua New Guinea, the Philippines, Solomon Islands and Timor-Leste. With three-quarters of the world's coral species and a third of the world's reef fishes found in its waters, the Coral Triangle is considered the centre of marine diversity on the planet. But the area is vast — too large to cover in a single story. My photographer friends David Doubilet and Jennifer Hayes chose the Philippines, the apex of the triangle, as their focus, and I joined them there.

The Philippines itself is no small destination. The country's 110 million people are spread across some 2000 islands. An additional 5600 islands are uninhabited. The Philippines ranks second to Indonesia as the most island-rich archipelago on earth, with 60 per cent of its people living on the coast and relying on the sea.

Its seas were once a bountiful provider. That is no longer the case. In the islands I visited I found a human struggle and a marine tragedy, each linked to the other. I learned a Filipino phrase that expresses starkly the desperation of the poor: 'kapit sa patalim', 'to grasp the blade'. It was explained to me like this: someone is in the water, drowning. I don't have a rope to throw them. All I have is a knife. I offer the blade of a knife to hold on to.

Filipino fishers are grasping the blade. Many resort to dangerous and destructive methods to glean food from depleted reefs. They use explosives, cyanide and fine-mesh nets through which none but the smallest fish can pass. All of these practices have been outlawed, but all are still in use. They are a cumulative disaster for coral reefs. The damage they inflict reduces the capacity of reefs to support life. The reefs' ecological heartbeat fades to a flicker.

One of the most degraded marine areas in the Philippines is the Danajon Bank, east of the island of Cebu in the central Philippines. Blast fishing using homemade grenades has been rampant here. It is estimated that a quarter of the fish caught in Danajon comes from illegal and destructive fishing methods.

I hired a boat to take me to reefs that had been subjected to this kind of fishing — though 'fishing' seems an inappropriate word for the practice of throwing a bomb at a reef and collecting the dead.

I slipped into the water and found myself in a wasteland of rubble, the pulverised remains of a coral reef. Its barrenness startled me. Elsewhere in the Philippines I had been dazzled by a jewel box of underwater splendour: corals every colour of the rainbow and creatures beyond counting. This reef was a graveyard populated by refugees. I saw a cleaner wrasse, a fish whose ecological role is to clean other fish, nibbling parasites and marine hitchhikers from their bodies with the dedication and delicacy of a preening bird. But this cleaner had no one to clean. It swam in apocalyptic solitude.

The corals around it lay toppled like trees after a hurricane. Among the dead stumps something flashed in the light and I picked up the bottom of a broken glass bottle, the remains of a fishing bomb. I had seen bottles like this filled with nitrate fertiliser and topped with a detonator. Light the fuse, count to three, then throw the device into the sea. Throw too soon and the dynamite might not detonate. Throw too late and you might lose a hand, an arm or a life.

I saw a figure in the distance, gleaning among the bomb-cratered ruins, and swam to meet him. He was wearing a long-sleeved shirt, trousers and a black hood over his head with holes for eyes and mouth. He had a battered pair of goggles over his eyes and pieces of plywood strapped to his feet for fins.

'Jellyfish?' I asked, pointing to his hood. My boat driver had told me of tangling with a box jellyfish in these waters. He had just had time to scream for help before passing out from the pain of the stinging tentacles. He showed me the welts on his arm and stomach, still vivid after 15 years.

'No, sun,' the diver answered. To collect enough food for his family, he said, he often had to stay out half a day in the burning heat, combing the reefs. He towed a battered polystyrene box to hold whatever he caught: whelks, abalone, sea urchins, crabs, fish if he was lucky. He used a hook in one hand and a spear in the other, poking, prodding, levering and hacking at the coral for any living thing that might be lurking there. He hadn't inflicted this damage; he was scavenging in the wake of those who had.

I watched him work. There was a sudden puff of black ink as he speared a cuttlefish. He picked up a sea cucumber and handed the warty creature to me. A tassel of white threads adorned its rear end. Quicker than I could register, the threads shot out and wrapped around my hand, sticking to my skin like superglue — the animal's reaction to being threatened. In the wild, after responding to a provocation with a sticky net, the cucumber crawls away. I detached the creature, and it went into the catch box.

The gleaner's laborious search for food is common practice

across the Philippines, and throughout the Coral Triangle, as ever-increasing numbers of people hunt for ever-decreasing quantities of seafood. Unsustainable fishing pressure has degraded more than 80 per cent of reefs in the Philippines. In the lean months of the year, gleaners gather an average of 250 grams of seafood an hour from the impoverished reefs. I watched this man suck another breath, flail his plywood fins and descend.

On the reefs of Palawan, an elongated island on the western border of the Philippines, I joined a group of men who were using a fishing technique known as pa-aling, in which divers drape a long net across a coral reef and scare fish into it. A compressor pumps air to the divers through narrow plastic tubing. It's a hazardous operation. The air is unfiltered, the compressors usually ancient and held together with wire and tape. Dive times and depths are only vaguely monitored, so the risk of contracting the bends is constant.

An earlier version of this type of fishing, muro-ami, now banned, involved children diving to the seabed and bashing the reef with rocks or metal bars to flush fish from crevices and drive them into a net. Many children were crippled from the bends or were entangled in nets and drowned.

I had never seen fishing like this before: half a dozen divers clamping air tubes between their teeth, wearing a motley assortment of goggles, masks and homemade fins, tucking the net between coral heads. It takes some skill to breathe through a tube not much wider than a drinking straw — breathing in from one side of your mouth and out from the other. When I tried it, I sucked from the wrong side and came up spluttering.

They were catching a few fish — I saw a scorpionfish, some mackerel-shaped species that I couldn't identify, a unicornfish, trapped by its horn. But the corals were clearly suffering — and from more than the physical damage caused by the fishing technique. The water temperature was 31°C, which exceeds the threshold at which coral polyps expel the symbiotic algae that gives them their kaleidoscopic colours, producing the effect known as coral bleaching. Among the living corals were many that were iceberg white — they looked as if they had been sculpted from marble. Others had streams of slime wafting from their dying heads.

It was strangely quiet. The usual reef symphony of crackling, popping, scratching and gnawing was muted. I was swimming through a sepulchral world of stressed, diseased and dying corals, from which other creatures had largely disappeared.

Marine scientists warn that worse is in store. Warming seas, acidifying seas, rising seas — these are the dark shadows that fall across all the world's coral reefs now. Of these, warming is the most immediate threat. Mass coral bleaching events used to occur once every few decades. Now the rate is once every six years. As the concentration of atmospheric carbon dioxide continues to increase, bleaching is likely to happen every year, with grave implications for reef health, indeed their very existence. In 2018, a report on the Great Barrier Reef predicted that within 15 years mass bleaching events would be so common that they would 'effectively sign the death certificate of one of the world's largest living marine structures'.

The reef threat isn't from rising temperatures alone. Recent measurements show that since the beginning of the industrial period some 250 years ago, the acidity of tropical surface waters has increased by 30 per cent. Laboratory experiments with corals suggest that the rate at which they produce their carbonate skeletons could decrease by a third over the next three to five decades. Reefs will reach a tipping point where the carbonate coral structure starts to dissolve faster than it can be formed. When that happens, reefs will begin to disintegrate. The most diverse ecosystem in the ocean — a planetary feature for 240 million years — will start to disappear.

Can this dystopian story have a different ending? Or at least be delayed? I believe so. Marine research has consistently revealed strong links between diversity, stability and productivity in ecosystems ranging from seagrass meadows and kelp forests to coral reefs. A diverse ecosystem is a resilient ecosystem, one that is able to rebound from environmental knocks, such as bleaching episodes, and from the pressures of human exploitation, such as overfishing. Depleted ecosystems lack this capacity. Their ability to recover from disturbances is diminished by their loss of biological richness.

One way to preserve diversity and sustain ecological functioning is to set aside areas of the sea as no-take reserves. The prohibition on harvesting from reserves is vital. It is now well established that fishing upsets the finely balanced ecology of a coral reef. If herbivorous fish are removed, for example, fast-growing seaweeds can gain a foothold and overwhelm the much slower growing coral. Algae also preclude settlement of new corals. If a coral reef turns into an algal reef, a multitude of species adapted to the coral ecosystem are displaced.

By contrast, no-take marine reserves restore reef health by replenishing biodiversity. The Philippines has been a world leader in creating such reserves. The approach was pioneered by Angel Alcala, a Filipino biologist who switched his attention from studying his country's reptiles and amphibians to conserving the fish stocks of its coral reefs. With colleagues at Silliman University — a private research institute in the city of Dumaguete — and in Australia, Angel experimented with the idea of creating small no-take marine reserves that could be managed by communities for their benefit.

Although the prime reason for creating marine reserves is to preserve biodiversity, for Angel the focus was their fisheries' benefit. 'Filipino people are fish eaters,' Angel, now in his nineties, told me when I met him at the research centre he leads at Silliman. 'They eat fish three times a day. To maintain that, there need to be marine reserves.'

Angel knows this not just theoretically, but personally. He grew up in a coastal village in a family that depended on the ocean for food. He remembers the pristine state of the reefs he saw as a boy in the 1930s. 'So beautiful. Full of all kinds of fish. The picture is still clear in my mind.' That picture is his inspiration and vision.

Angel started in the early 1980s with two prototype reserves: one at an island that was inhabited (Apo, 25 kilometres south of Dumaguete), and one at an island that was not (Sumilon, near the southern tip of Cebu). From the beginning, all forms of harvesting were prohibited. 'When we say "marine protected area" we mean no-take. No ifs or buts,' Angel said.

The results were impressive. In 10 years the biomass of some fish species in the reserves increased at least sixfold. As the density of fish inside the reserves increased, fishers reaped the benefit through the phenomenon of spillover: individual fish 'spill over' the reserves' boundaries into waters where they can legally be caught. The idea that no-take sanctuaries could replenish fish stocks on nearby exploited reefs offered a bright speck of hope in an otherwise dismal outlook for coastal fishers.

But in the early years that hope wasn't obvious to Apo's residents, and even though the sanctuary area was only a quarter of the island's fringing reef, many islanders opposed the closing of traditional fishing grounds. It was the women of Apo who caught Angel's vision of what the reserve could achieve. They became its staunchest defenders, stationing themselves on the beach to watch for trespassers as they minded their children and wove mats and baskets for sale.

They were the forerunners of the bantay dagat, municipally appointed sea wardens who guard the 1600 or so marine reserves that have been created in Apo's wake. Had it not been for these women, it is likely that the sanctuary boundaries would have been breached, and the fisheries benefit of the reserve would never have been realised.

Nor would the tourism benefit have transpired. Today, sightseers and divers flock to the island, paying a visitor levy to do so. A third of the levy goes to the community for needs such as subsidised electricity, livelihood assistance and transportation.

Mary Aldeon, one of the original reserve defenders, runs a homestay. She summarised Apo's success to me: 'Many livelihoods, many guests, many income.' Some residents operate guesthouses, some rent masks and snorkels, some sell T-shirts. I bought one with a shoal of turtles printed on the back. Thirty years ago, turtles were unknown at Apo, Mary told me. 'God sent the turtles,' she said. The people created a safe haven for them.

On one of the outside walls of Mary's house someone had painted a mural of a shoal of jacks, a desirable catch for Filipino fishers. I remarked on the painted fish to Mary. 'Apo Island lives if they live,' she said. And live they do, with much else besides.

I swam with Apo's turtles a few metres from the island's main beach, floating above them and drenching my eyes in the starburst patterns of browns, greens and blacks on their shells. I thought of them as swimming mandalas, carrying their origin story on their backs. Fat green parrotfish finned through the coral meadows. Such fish are rare on unprotected reefs.

Apo Island's success caught the attention of Rodrigo Alanano when he was elected mayor of the municipality of Dauin, on the adjacent coast of Negros Island, in 2001. He immediately set out to increase the number of marine protected areas (MPAs) along Dauin's coastline. He could do this because municipalities have jurisdiction over their coastal waters out to 15 kilometres.

When I called on Rodrigo to ask about his advocacy for protected areas I found him watering strawberry plants in his yard. I asked him how he had convinced the subsistence fishers of his municipality to give up a portion of their fishing waters.

'I told them we needed to have breeding grounds as well as fishing grounds,' he said. 'I told them, "If you have a sanctuary, populations will grow and some fishes will get out of the sanctuary, and those ones are for you. The reserve will be a breeding ground for fishes now and forever, for you and for the future." Later on, I told them it would become a diving spot, and there would be an income from that.'

Still, persuading fishers to accept an immediate loss for an uncertain future gain was no easy matter. The average annual income for Dauin's 23,000 people is a few hundred New Zealand dollars. Many residents opposed the sanctuaries. Rodrigo was served lawsuits and received death threats. He shrugged at the memory. 'When I became mayor I gave my life for this profession,' he said.

'What made you so passionate?' I asked. 'You're not even from a fishing family.'

'I am a mining engineer,' he replied. 'I worked for mining companies for twelve years before entering politics. We destroyed mountains. We used toxic chemicals that flowed out to sea. I am an experienced destroyer of the environment. I am licensed to destroy. What I experienced is that once you destroy the environment, no human being can put that right again. It cannot be put back for your children. And when you kill the last fish you will realise you can't eat money.'

Rodrigo's arguments prevailed, and during his time as mayor he increased the number of MPAs along Dauin's coastline from four to nine. I dived in some of them. Though small, they protect wondrous creatures. At one site I watched in hypnotic awe as the slender bodies of garden eels rose from their holes in the seabed and swayed as if to the music of a snake charmer. There must have been thousands of them, each the thickness of a thumb and more than half a metre tall. If I waved a hand, in an instant the entire colony would withdraw into their holes. A few minutes later they would cautiously emerge and rise up again, cocking their heads into the current like question marks.

Nearby, in the sunken wreck of a fishing boat, I saw a swarm of juvenile convict blennies. These boldly patterned eel-shaped fish build elaborate networks of tunnels and chambers into which the adults retire, never leaving their labyrinth, even to feed. They work continuously on their constructions, sucking up sand with their mouths, swimming to the tunnel entrances and spitting out the spoil. The 'convict' part of their name comes from the black-and-white bar pattern on their bodies

— though it's a stretch to make that connection.

Other strange crew in that underwater wreck were a sad-eyed lionfish, flexing its gaudy red-and-white barred pectorals, and a species of cardinal with violet lips and matching streaks under its eyes. Nearby, a pair of Moorish idols nibbled at the biological fuzz on a pile of tyres. 'Moorish idol' is one of those fish names that give no clues. If anything, the name is a misdirection. These fish are not found anywhere near the homeland of the Moors, in North Africa. They are an Indo-Pacific species. Disc-shaped, deeper than they are long, they are so compressed they look like they've been rolled out like pastry. The vertical lemon, white and black bars make them one of the most striking fish on the reef. Their mouth is at the end of a tubular snout, and from their dorsal fin trails a long white filament that stretches past their tail. As if that weren't sufficient adornment, there are two small horns in front of the eyes.

As the pioneers of marine protection foresaw, such creatures are a drawcard for tourists, and Dauin's MPAs have become popular dive destinations, as have hundreds of other sites across the Philippines. Most of Dauin's reserves are referred to by the names of the fish species that serve as their celebrity attractions: Nemo/Clown Fish MPA, Mandarin MPA, Frog Fish MPA, Ghost Pipe and Sea Horse MPA.

As tourism has flourished, fishers have seen opportunities to switch from catching fish to providing services. Near Puerto Galera, 'port of galleons', on the island of Mindoro, I watched snorkellers being towed out to see giant clams by fishers in small outrigger canoes powered by chainsaw and lawnmower engines.

In Dauin, several fishers have retrained as dive masters. Amado A. Alar II runs Bongo Bongo Divers, down a sideroad from the Chooks To Go fried chicken house. He told me that when Dauin's MPAs were being established, some fishers refused to accept the loss of their fishing grounds. They cut the ropes of the buoys that marked the sanctuary boundaries, slipped into the protected area at night to catch fish, and came to blows with the bantay dagat if they were caught.

But when they saw their catches increase, they changed their tune. 'Slowly, slowly the people understand — "Ah, that's why it is like this",' said Alar. 'Now they will protect the sanctuary if they see someone fishing there. They understand that we have a nursery here.'

The nursery effect is considered one of the key benefits of MPA networks. Larval fish disperse from reefs in protected areas to unprotected reefs, providing replenishment.

Rene Abesamis, one of Angel Alcala's colleagues at Silliman, has studied the process in Dauin's MPAs. He chose the vagabond butterflyfish, a species with a larval phase of around four weeks, for the research, and found that its larvae can drift up to 40 kilometres in monsoon winds and currents before settling into a new reef habitat.

Knowing that fish on your local reef may have come from sanctuaries 40 kilometres away has a powerful effect on people, Rene told me. 'It tells them that even if they live in different municipal entities, they belong to the same ecological network. It tells them their efforts are connected.'

Mutual replenishment is the logic behind efforts to scale up MPAs into a nationwide network, and to fill gaps between them. The connection between reef protection and fish productivity is now so well accepted that Philippines law stipulates that 15 per cent of coastal municipal waters must be protected within no-take MPAs. But the establishment of a reserve is no guarantee of its effectiveness. Most are tiny and not well managed, Angel told me — mere 'paper parks'. And the cumulative area of protection is not great.

'Only three per cent of our coral reefs are protected so far,' Angel said. 'We need twenty to thirty per cent.' It's a matter of empowering local communities, he added, and giving them the resources to protect the investment they have made. Even sanctuaries that are properly cared for by their local communities are susceptible to poaching by outsiders.

Poaching is a growing problem across the Philippines. Poachers with fast boats and scuba gear can strip a sanctuary in a night, Darrell Pasco told me on the island of Siquijor, east of Dauin. Darrell works in coastal resource management for the province. One of Siquijor's MPAs was poached four times in a single year. The intruders come at night, during fiestas, or at times of bad weather, when there will be fewer eyes watching, he says. They carry weapons. How can Siquijor's bantay dagat, who earn less than 10 dollars a month, oppose such people? 'All we are doing is giving the poachers more fish,' one resident complained.

Siquijor is known as an island of mystery and magic, of witchcraft and faith healers. But it will take more than faith to heal the island's ailing fisheries. High-value fish have become scarce, while species that were formerly considered trash fish have become culinary staples. Damselfish — darting cobalt-blue beauties with mango-dipped tails — were never eaten, Darrell said. Now they sell for a dollar a kilogram in the market. I saw them there alongside such delicacies as sea anemones cooked in coconut milk, spider conch, sea cucumbers, sea urchins, and seaweeds that looked like clusters of green pearls.

I saw the struggle Siquijor's fishers have when I slipped into the silky sea one morning to watch a group of men haul up a bubu, or fish trap, from the seabed 75 metres below. Slowly it rose, a 5-metre-long woven basket spacious enough that I could have swum pirouettes inside it. The pattern of its bamboo weave was intricate, the work of skilled hands for untold hours. As seven men heaved it onto the deck of their banca — the traditional double-outrigger boat of the Philippines — I peered inside, looking for the harvest of fish that should have been there, for the baited trap had lain on the seabed for a week. A fisherman reached in and lifted out a single triggerfish — a meagre return for a week's deployment.

The next bubu I watched being hauled up had no fish at all. 'Mingaw,' one fisherman called as the trap broke the surface. 'Empty.' I winced as small jellyfish and broken arms of sea anemones falling from the trap stung my skin. And I winced for the dashed expectations of the men and their families. Bubu fishers may earn as little as a dollar per trap per week. Their households are typically on or below the poverty line, as is 60 per cent of the country's coastal population.

Like Dauin's mayor Rodrigo, Darrell has been threatened over his efforts to expand MPAs and deter poaching. To guard the property, he keeps a watchdog and sleeps in a hut outside his house. 'I'm afraid for my security and my family's security, but I'm still doing my job,' he told me.

There is no other option, he says. 'We have to give an honest and profound education for every Filipino that it is up to us to take care of the ocean, because we get almost everything we need from the ocean. If we don't do that, the time will come when we will have no more fish to catch, and we will only see fish in books and on the internet, not in the ocean.'

Tourism helps alleviate pressure on dwindling fish stocks, but not every place can be a dive hotspot. Another way of relieving the demand on reef ecosystems is for fishers to take up alternative livelihoods such as seaweed farming or sea cucumber farming. At a remote atoll in the Sulu Sea I met families living on bamboo platforms in reef lagoons, drying seaweed. The algae they farm produces carrageenan, a polysaccharide used as a stabiliser in medicines, toothpaste, pill capsules, cosmetics and other products. Thousands of Filipino families have become seaweed ranchers.

In the islands of the Calamian group, at the northern tip of Palawan, people are learning how to ranch sea cucumbers. I helped release dozens of juvenile sea cucumbers the size of my little finger from net cages so they could free-range across warm estuarine flats. In two months they will reach the size of fat sausages. When dried, sea cucumbers fetch 10 times the price of grouper.

All such initiatives reduce fishing pressure on reefs, and it is beyond question that reefs regenerate when human pressure is removed. The preeminent dive site in the Philippines, Tubbataha Reefs, a national park and World Heritage Site that lies in the centre of the Sulu Sea, is evidence of this. Here I saw barrel sponges large enough to curl up inside. When they spawn, these giant animals appear to smoke like volcanoes. I watched confetti clouds of fish — orange, purple, green, yellow — floating above coral trees, while grey reef sharks slept on coral sand beneath. I saw creamy sea fans so intricate they looked like a Japanese woodcut. A well-camouflaged octopus unspooled its arms and, with an instantaneous colour change from fawn to charcoal, jetted away.

Exceptional today, these reefs were all but destroyed by dynamite fishing in the 1960s. Strict enforcement of no-take rules has redeemed them. But will they survive bleaching and other climate pressures? Most researchers think not. It is projected that by 2050 more than 90 per cent of the Coral Triangle's reefs will be critically threatened by climate impacts. As reefs fail, food insecurity in the region will become calamitous. How will coastal dwellers survive?

Forty years ago, the movie *Apocalypse Now* was filmed in the Philippines. The Philippines has stared into its own apocalyptic future of degraded reefs and depleted seas. Many of its people have recognised the choice they must make: seize the moment of change, or grasp the blade of crisis. Over the past four decades, communities have made hard choices to forgo fishing everywhere for the ability to catch fish somewhere. They have discovered that visitors will pay to see flourishing reefs and the creatures that live on them. They have become guardians and stewards of an incomparable ocean realm.

But these changes alone will not preserve the reefs on which millions depend. Ocean warming is locked in. Ocean acidification is locked in. Extreme weather and food insecurity are certainties. What can local efforts achieve in the face of intractable planetary change?

I posed this question to coral reef biologist Wilfredo Licuanan, a professor at Manila's De La Salle University. He said it was a matter of buying time. 'We have to delay the inevitable long enough for some solution to come up that is not yet visible,' he said. Reef stewardship through marine protection buys time for the Philippines economy to shift from extraction to other modes of production. It buys time for the international community to begin to deliver just compensation to nations such as the Philippines, which have contributed least to global warming, but are its most immediate victims. And it buys time for the climate reckoning that each of us must face.

For Wilfredo, the important thing was not to give in to despair. 'I want to be able to at least look my students in the eye and say, "I'm trying",' he said. 'If I fail, I don't give up, I try again.'

What marine reserves are showing in the Philippines and around the world is that even small conservation efforts can help restore the biodiversity that has been drained from the natural world by unconstrained human exploitation. Restored biological richness increases ecosystem stability and improves the likelihood that ecosystems will withstand environmental shocks. Marine reserves are an insurance policy societies take out as earth systems falter.

They are necessary, but they are not sufficient for replenishing and sustaining the ocean, in the same way as planting trees is necessary but not sufficient for reversing earth's warming climate. Stewardship is required not just for the areas of coastline and ocean that communities and countries choose to keep free of extraction. An ethic of stewardship and accountability is required for all oceans, as it is for land and atmosphere. Ultimately, we all face the same choice: seize the day, or grasp the blade.

Song of
rising isles

I AM WALKING ACROSS THE Greenland tundra, verdant and lush in midsummer, sliced by meltwater streams that tumble to the sea. Butterflies flutter up from pink and purple wildflowers, and the fluffy heads of cottonflower, white as the snow on the surrounding mountains, toss in the warm wind. It is unseasonably warm, and I have stripped down to T-shirt and jeans. I pity the sled dogs that pace, whine and doze in their enclosures. Are they dreaming of endless winter darkness and the joy of ice?

I am with a *National Geographic* expedition cruise around southern Greenland. This July weekend has set a record for the amount of meltwater flowing off the Greenland ice sheet: 7.2 million Olympic swimming pools' worth of water. I cannot envisage such a volume of water. I do a quick calculation: the weekend's ice melt would raise the level of Lake Taupō by 30 metres. This I can grasp, and it startles me.

A few days ago our group circled in inflatable boats around icebergs that were the colour of sapphires. The colour arises from the immense pressure of the glacier having squeezed the air out of the ice. As the glacier retreats — and most of Greenland's glaciers are in retreat — this blue ice comes out of the glacial depths and shears off into the sea. We approached the face of the glacier to watch it calve. There was a puff of grit and ice as a slab of glacier fell into the sea, and a few seconds later came the sound, like gunshot.

It is one thing to know from temperature data that the Arctic is warming faster than almost anywhere on earth, but to experience a landscape in transition — retreating glaciers, fjords choked with glacial ice, a melting ice sheet — gives a palpable immediacy to this critical moment in earth's history. It sharply focuses the connection between the inflow of meltwater to the oceans here and in the Antarctic and its impacts thousands of kilometres away, in the South Pacific. It is there, on the atolls of Tuvalu and Kiribati, that my understanding of sea-level rise has taken shape.

Atolls entrance me. Whenever I have flown across the Pacific my forehead has been pressed to the aircraft's window, hoping for a glimpse of a pool of turquoise in a radiant blue ocean — an atoll lagoon. Around its rim, palm-covered islets, each with a halo of ivory sand and a smoke ring of cloud floating above like piped meringue. I marvel at their tenuous perch on the lip of an ancient volcano that rises from the seabed kilometres below. Truly, as the late I-Kiribati poet Teweiariki (Tevi) Teaero wrote, they are garlands of the gods.

I visited Kiribati in 2016 for a *National Geographic* special issue on climate change. Kiribati, the Marshall Islands, Tokelau, Tuvalu and the Maldives are all nations made up predominantly of low-lying atolls, and all are at risk of becoming uninhabitable as a warming climate drives sea levels upwards. Kiribati itself has 32 low atolls — and just one high island — in an expanse of the central Pacific larger than India.

I had already written about Kiribati's neighbour and former colonial twin, Tuvalu, in a story on rising seas for *New Zealand Geographic* in 2004. For decades, Tuvalu had been a favourite location for canary-in-the-coalmine media reports on rising seas and disappearing islands. Story after story dramatised Tuvalu's supposedly imminent demise, with headlines such as 'Tuvalu Toodle-oo', 'The Canary is Drowning' and 'Tuvalu Sinks Today — The Rest of Us Tomorrow?'. Tuvalu was persistently portrayed as the poster child of a planetary crisis, the innocent victim of the West's appetite for carbon.

A prominent US environmental campaigner had declared that Tuvalu's leaders had 'conceded defeat in their battle with the rising sea, announcing that they will abandon their homeland' — a claim that would be repeated a few years later in Al Gore's *An Inconvenient Truth*. 'The evacuation and shutting down of a nation has begun,' reported the *Guardian*. I wanted to find out how much of this hyperbolic reporting was true, and how much was fiction.

Mostly fiction, it transpired. In Tuvalu's capital, Funafuti, it was business as usual. Government staff were about to move in to a brand-new building overlooking the lagoon. The country's first cellphone tower had just been erected. Tuvalu was enjoying a windfall profit from the sale of its 'dot tv' internet suffix. There was a conspicuous absence of alarmed Tuvaluans looking to evacuate a disappearing homeland. It appeared that reports of the nation's demise, like those of Mark Twain's death, had been greatly exaggerated.

Yet the output of hand-wringing stories, broadcasts, book chapters and documentaries with doom-laden titles and dire prognostications of island extinction has continued unabated. Writers, filmmakers, broadcasters and 'influencers' continue to contemplate with grim fascination the annihilation of low-lying atoll archipelagos such as Tuvalu.

Australian social anthropologist Carol Farbotko has coined the term 'wishful sinking' to describe the melodramatic reporting of sea-level rise. Media and their consumers view from a comfortable distance the spectacle of island states doing battle with a belligerent ocean. They watch 'partly in horror and partly with perverse impatience for the first islands to disappear'. Only after they sink beneath the waves are the islands 'useful as an absolute truth of the urgency of climate change, and thus a prompt to save the rest of the planet'.

Low-lying atolls as the sacrificial lamb that goads the world into action? It's a troubling thought: Pacific people cast as victims in an environmental horror movie, helplessly fleeing a devouring ocean. There is even a climate-change-disaster tourism twist, with vulnerable atolls promoted as places to see before they disappear.

But are they, in fact, disappearing?

I returned to Tuvalu in 2014 to see what had changed during 10 more years of rising seas. From the air, Funafuti's main island, Fongafale, looks like a triangular green kite with two long tails. Its total land area is about a tenth the size of Rangitoto Island in Auckland's Hauraki Gulf. Half of Tuvalu's population of 12,000 lives there.

I stepped off the plane into the sweltering heat and humidity of hurricane season. Walking to the guesthouse, I smelled the familiar floral fragrance of frangipani and the pungent passionfruit aroma of ripe breadfruit. A stream of Tuvaluans puttered past on motor scooters, the national vehicle.

The place was much as I remembered it. No one was queuing to leave. New businesses were opening. Fongafale's population had increased by 1500 since my previous visit, and the national population was increasing by around 1 per cent per year. So much for the shutting down of a nation.

Fongafale might not have changed, but my perception of the sea-level threat had undergone some modification after reading just-published research by Paul Kench, a geomorphologist at the University of Auckland. According to the research, Tuvalu wasn't sinking, or even shrinking — it was growing. This despite the fact the sea level in Tuvalu's part of the Pacific has been rising at a rate of around 5 millimetres per year, roughly twice the global average — a cumulative rise of 15 centimetres since 1971.

Paul's analysis of all 101 islands in the Tuvalu atoll chain found that Tuvalu's land area had increased by almost 3 per cent (74 hectares). Only one of those 101 islands had suffered the predicted fate of the entire country and was now under water.

The same was true for other atoll nations. Paul told me that he and his colleagues had analysed more than 600 coral reef islands in the Pacific and Indian oceans, and that around 80 per cent of them had either remained stable or increased in size (roughly 40 per cent in each category), while only 20 per cent had shown the net reduction that is widely assumed to be an island's fate when sea level rises. Some islands grew by 5 hectares in a decade.

When the researchers compared modern aerial photographs of the islands of Tuvalu's main atoll, Funafuti, with detailed maps made during scientific expeditions in the 1890s, they found that the islands had gained 30 hectares.

But the result that surprised the researchers most, Paul told

me, is not that islands can increase in size as sea level rises —
important and counterintuitive as that is — but the extent to
which they move around on their reef platforms. Two-thirds
of the islands in the study migrated lagoonward as their ocean-
side coastlines eroded and sediment accreted on the side facing
the lagoon. One of Funafuti's 33 reef islands had shifted more
than 100 metres in 40 years.

How could this be — an outcome so contrary to prevailing
assumptions?

What I learned from Paul is that far from being static and
at the mercy of rising seas, coral atolls are among the most
dynamic landforms on earth.

I hired an open boat and made a spray-drenched trip across
Funafuti's 275-square-kilometre lagoon in the teeth of a
rising westerly. The boatman's face glistened with salt water as
he steered through a labyrinth of fringing reefs and coral heads
to the uninhabited island of Tepuka, and nosed in to shore. I
waded to the beach and picked up a handful of coarse coral
gravel, noting the hundreds of different shapes and sizes of the
grains. Maybe I wasn't holding infinity in the palm of my hand,
but I was holding the stuff of islands.

Reef islands such as Tepuka are perpetual construction
sites. Their surrounding coral reefs are the factories that
produce the raw building material: calcium carbonate, the
same raw material as cement, the foundation of the human
construction industry.

The factory workers are the biological agents that turn the
skeletons of corals and other carbonate-containing creatures
into sediment. Fish, sea urchins and sponges are the principal

processors. Collectively, they can produce 20 kilograms of sediment per square metre of reef per year. Any reef snorkeller who has watched parrotfish nibbling coral and excreting grit will recognise just how productive these workers can be.

Molluscs, calcium-secreting algae and foraminifera add to the sediment supply. Some of Tepuka's beaches have an orange hue from the abundance of washed-up foraminifera skeletons.

In my conversations with Paul Kench, he spoke of an island's carbonate budget — its sedimentary profit-and-loss account. On the income side of the ledger is the rubble, gravel and sand produced by the reef ecosystem or imported into it by storms, for instance. On the expenditure side is sediment lost through being eroded to microscopic fineness, dissolved in seawater or exported by waves or currents into the deep ocean.

The budget can be more or less balanced for decades, centuries, even millennia, and then experience a sudden blowout. In 1972, Cyclone Bebe hit Tuvalu, depositing overnight a 20-kilometre ridge of coral rubble that was more than 3 metres high. In the following years, that material was worked into the matrix of several reef islands on the southeastern side of Funafuti — the side that took the brunt of Bebe's force. That one cyclone increased the land area of Funafuti by 10 per cent.

Tepuka, on the western rim of the atoll, missed out on the Bebe deposit, and is one of a handful of Funafuti's islands that have been shrinking in size. I walked to the ocean side of the island, where toppled trunks of coconut palms lay crisscrossed like knitting needles. A metre-high scarp of sandy soil hard up against the vegetation showed where wave action was scouring away the land.

I had seen this kind of erosion on coastlines elsewhere in the world, and had written about it in a *New Zealand Geographic* story on rising seas. For that story I visited Mōkau, on the Taranaki coast of New Zealand, to ask residents about their experience of land lost to the sea. Their stories were grim. One storm in 2011 had lowered the beach by 5 metres in two days. Another had sliced 10 horizontal metres off the face of a coastal cliff on which people's homes are built. I saw a Norfolk pine tilting at a crazy angle, ready to fall. I saw fences hanging in midair and danger tape where the seaward edges of properties were crumbling away.

Residents have been doing what they can to hold back the tide, bolstering the coast with tyres, ponga logs, road matting, wool bales filled with gravel. They pointed out where baches had been pulled down when they got too close to the cliff edge. In other parts of the country, I'd seen them left to topple into the sea.

In Ōamaru, I climbed over a barrier fence to walk what remained of a coastal road. It's disorienting to follow a white-painted centreline that leads into thin air — great chunks of asphalt gone, as if bitten clean off by a shark. I watched dull green curlers lick the stony beach 6 metres below the road. Storms had tossed gravel and stones onto what remained of the tarmac. What road could withstand that level of wave action?

In all these places, I assumed that the loss of coastline and beach was irreversible. But Paul's work on coral reef islands offers a different reality of swings and roundabouts: abrasion on one side of an island, accretion on the other, with entire islands shifting on their reef platforms in dynamic response to wind, waves and sea level. In Tepuka's case, a net loss in area of 22 per cent since 1896 is only part of the story. The island has undergone an almost constant reworking of its sedimentary material over the past century. It has grown longer (by 150 metres) and narrower (by 110 metres), and its position has rotated clockwise on the reef.

Although it is shrinking now, a big enough storm could push Tepuka's sediment budget back into the black. It has happened here before. Surveys across the island have shown that large sections have been overwashed by the sea, with tonnes of sediment deposited on top of the existing vegetation.

The message of Tepuka, in Paul's view, is that it is as important to focus on what sediment is doing as on what sea level is doing.

Tepuka is important for another reason. Dating of the island's core has shown that it is a very young island, formed between 500 and 1000 years ago. Tuvaluans, whose occupation of the islands goes back more than 2000 years, might well have watched it grow.

That young age is significant because it lies within a period of steady sea levels — an epoch the planet is just leaving. It had been thought that islands couldn't form during such periods; that falling sea levels were needed to trigger the processes of island-building. Tepuka shows otherwise, and work conducted by Paul and his colleagues in the Marshall Islands has shown that reef islands can form even when sea level is rising rapidly.

Sediment analysis on Jabat Island, in the Marshall Islands, reveals that it started forming nearly 5000 years ago, when the oceans were rising to a peak more than a metre higher than today's sea level (a point that may be reached again by the end of this century, according to predictions by the Intergovernmental Panel on Climate Change). Coarse sediments in Jabat's core indicate that the island began forming as a result of high-energy storm action — the very condition that is forecast to occur with greater frequency as the planet's atmosphere warms.

The Jabat findings suggest that if islands could form during periods of rising sea level and increased storm activity in the past, then there is no reason to think that they can't sustain themselves under the same circumstances today. Rising sea levels might reactivate processes of island building that have been relatively dormant during the long period of sea-level stability.

'The faster sea level goes up, the more dynamic these islands are going to appear,' Paul told me. Does this mean that predictions of atoll apocalypse are incorrect? That atolls will survive rising seas? The answer depends largely on what happens to coral reefs. At present, coral reefs, the source of the raw material of atolls, are suffering and dying. As the sea grows warmer and more acidic throughout this century, reef growth is predicted to slow and even stop. Warming seas kill coral by bleaching. Acidifying seas inhibit the ability of marine animals to build their carbonate skeletons.

In the short term, the loss of living coral on reefs could equate to a sediment gain for atoll islands. After a devastating coral bleaching event in 1998, when a sixth of the world's reefs are thought to have died, a huge repository of coral rubble became available for island building. If heat-stressed corals show increased mortality in coming decades, the sediment supply for islands is likely to increase.

But at some point unrelenting coral mortality will lead to reef disappearance. And where reefs go, islands must eventually follow. If the construction materials run out, building will cease. Dead reefs cannot maintain the islands they have built.

I was initially hesitant to report this research. Climate change denial was still rife in those years. I wanted to give no quarter to deniers or comfort to fence-sitters who made the spurious claim that 'the science isn't settled'. But neither was I happy with the alarmist narrative that atoll nations were about to be wiped off the face of the earth.

Paul and his fellow researchers felt that the assumption that islands would soon be uninhabitable was leading to poor planning decisions by island governments. Rather than exploring strategic measures they could take to adapt to new climate realities, governments were ramping up island defences such as reclamations and seawalls. These responses are costly and often maladaptive, Paul told me. They attempt to provide coastal protection in areas where it is unlikely to provide long-term benefit.

Paul believes atoll nations should adopt an approach of informed flexibility, adjusting infrastructure according to how their islands are changing. 'If countries are serious about maintaining their sovereignty and viability, then they have to confront some hard questions about how they plan and adapt. What frustrates me is these countries know so little about their islands. They don't even know how high they are. They'll have really good maps of land ownership, but they can't tell you how an island's changed or shifted over time. If they had land planning units that collected data on changing island morphology — the sort of information we've been gathering on Tuvalu — all of a sudden they've got a basis to say: these islands over here seem to be growing, or these ones seem to be eroding on this side but accreting on the other. You can make choices about where you're going to develop.'

'We don't say this will be easy,' he added. 'There are hurdles to overcome in terms of land tenure and other social factors. But we think the future lies in shifting infrastructure to one or more decentralised sites, rather than trying to defend the line on a single island. I'd rather hear the prime minister of Tuvalu or the president of Kiribati stand up and say to the international community, "We want to be here in a hundred years. We are facing enormous environmental challenges. Help us plan effectively."'

What appealed to me about Paul's thinking was its optimism and its respect for the agency of island people. The problem with the 'drowning islands' narrative is that it invites atoll islanders to think of themselves as climate victims destined to become stateless refugees. There is neither optimism nor agency in that view, and I didn't want its bleak assumptions to distort my coverage of Kiribati.

There is a kind of revolving-door climate journalism where reporters expect to see certain evidences of loss and damage (flooding at king tides, coastal erosion, breached seawalls, saltwater intrusion into gardens) and go looking for them, then report on what they find, perpetuating the cycle.

Kiribati and Tuvalu experience all these impacts, and they shouldn't be ignored. But they must be balanced by other observations, such as the geomorphologists' evidence that reef islands have either remained the same size or increased in size over the past four decades, thus demonstrating an ability to keep up with slowly rising seas. To extrapolate from king-tide damage to the imminent inhabitability of Pacific atolls is irresponsible journalism, but I have seen it time and again.

One of the worst examples has been the repeated claim that the Carteret Islands — seven islands scattered around the rim of a 25-kilometre-diameter atoll off the coast of Bougainville

— are being evacuated. Western media seized on the islands, traditionally known as Tulun or Kilinailau, as ground zero for the climate crisis. The Carteret islanders were said to be the world's first climate refugees. Evacuation was to be complete by 2007. That deadline came and went. A few families were moved, but, unhappy in their new homes in Bougainville among people with whom they had little in common, many returned to their home islands. In 2017 it was reported that the atoll population had almost doubled.

Rather than participate in the narrative of victimhood and powerlessness, I came to Kiribati with the words of Epeli Hau'ofa in my mind. In his writing and teaching he rejected the portrayal of the Pacific as weak, disconnected and dependent on outside help for survival — a soul-sapping belittlement that the Pacific has endured for centuries.

'What kind of teaching is it to stand in front of young people from your own region, people you claim as your own, who have come to university with high hopes for the future, and you tell them that our countries are hopeless?' he asked in a seminal essay published in 1994. 'Is this not what neocolonialism is all about? To make people believe that they have no choice but to depend?'

The title of Hau'ofa's essay, 'Our Sea of Islands', comes from one of his most cited ideas: that the Pacific should not be regarded as isolated specks of land in a vast and empty ocean, but rather as a magnificent web of islands connected by countless voyaging pathways. The first view — a European framing — puts the focus on tiny islands far from the centres of cultural relevance and political power. The second puts the emphasis on the expansive network that connects them. Pacific people, wrote Hau'ofa, 'were connected rather than separated by the sea. Far from being sea-locked peoples marooned on coral or volcanic tips of land, islanders formed an oceanic community based on voyaging.'

Smallness is a state of mind, he wrote. He refused to accept that state. He wrote about what he called his 'road to Damascus' experience on the Big Island of Hawai'i. It seemed, in a single moment, to sum up all that was wrong about belittling and patriarchal attitudes towards the Pacific — attitudes that reeked of colonial snobbery. He was watching red-hot magma flow from a volcano. Its power was unchallengeable. 'Under the aegis of Pele, and before my very eyes, the Big Island was growing, rising from the depths of a mighty sea,' he wrote. 'The world of Oceania is not small; it is huge and growing bigger every day.'

'Oceania' was Hau'ofa's favourite word for the Pacific, because it suggested a bigness of vision. 'Oceania is vast, Oceania is expanding, Oceania is hospitable and generous, Oceania is humanity rising from the depths of brine and regions of fire deeper still, Oceania is us. We are the sea, we are the ocean, we must wake up to this ancient truth . . . We must not allow anyone to belittle us again, and take away our freedom.'

I found the same rejection of implied weakness in the writings of Tevi Teaero. Rather than focus on sinking atolls, Tevi wanted to draw attention to a resurgent Pacific, islands of confidence in a sea of troubles. He urged the people of Kiribati and the Pacific to reach deep into their past to find solutions for the problems of the present.

I was initially sceptical about this call. A rapidly changing climate is a contemporary phenomenon (at least since humans have been on the planet) that surely requires contemporary technologies and approaches to solving it. But then I recalled that in the Pacific mind it is normal to seek ancestral answers to contemporary dilemmas.

This orientation towards the past is embedded in language through an intriguing dual usage of words relating to time and position. In the languages of Austronesia (a swathe of islands of the Pacific and Indian oceans that span from Rapanui in the east to Madagascar in the west) the word for past is the same as that for in front, and the word for the future is the same as behind.

Westerners have the opposite chronogeography. We speak of 'looking back' on the past and 'looking forward' to the future. Many of us peer anxiously into the fog of the future, seeking to know what it will bring. Life is full of projections, forecasts, prognoses and contingencies. Pacific peoples live differently. The future occupies them little and troubles them less. Why should the unknowable occupy the mind more than the knowable?

To a mind oriented in that way, it makes sense to respond to a threatening future by considering lessons from the past. One lesson history teaches is that island people possess depths of resilience and adaptability in the face of environmental challenge. 'I see adaptation as not just about seawalls but about revisiting our traditional knowledge systems,' Tevi told me when I visited him at his home on Tarawa, the main island of Kiribati. 'We need the collaboration of our international partners, but it must be an active collaboration, as people who are empowered to tackle our own problems.'

As much as anything, what Tevi called for was a return to cultural confidence, based in recollection of the voyaging heritage of Pacific peoples. The word for voyaging is 'borau', Tevi told me. The word for floating away is 'betinako'. Islanders have the impression that the outside world thinks they are powerless victims. That the elements — storms, droughts, rising seas — are in control.

'The world is telling us we are betinako,' Tevi said. 'I want to take a new approach.' By resurrecting indigenous ways, growing and preserving traditional foods, achieving food security, the people will grow in confidence and self-reliance, and will turn away from 'aidiction' — dependence on outside assistance.

Some of Tevi's ideas seem to be taking root. At a high school on Tarawa I sampled an array of traditional foods prepared by the students. Several were based on the fruit of the pandanus, which to I-Kiribati is the tree of life, since it provides not only food but also medicine, timber, thatch, weaving fibre, rope and even scented body oils. I-Kiribati have developed a great variety of ways to eat pandanus fruit, cooking it, pounding it into flour, and more. I often snacked on the raw fruit, which is as big as a volleyball, made up of hundreds of segments, green on the outside and sunrise-orange in the centre: you break them off and suck the sweet juice, spitting out the fibre.

The national greeting in Kiribati is 'Mauri!' The word has a slightly different meaning from what it means in te reo Māori, where it roughly translates to life force. To I-Kiribati, mauri has more the meaning of balance. If a person is in a state of mauri, they are healthy, protected and ready to face the world, Tevi explained. 'Being mauri means knowing and living the culture.'

I experienced several Kiribati traditions, and felt their depth and solidity. One afternoon I joined a group of fishermen travelling from Tarawa to its nearest atoll neighbour, Abaiang. It was a day so calm the clouds had blue-green bellies from the reflection of the sea. Midway through the 40-kilometre journey, the skipper cut the outboard motor at a certain reef and one of the crew threw hand-made cigarettes rolled in pandanus leaves into the sea as offerings and as a mark of respect for the owners of the territory we were crossing.

When we arrived at Abaiang, before we did anything else, my guide took me to a sacred site, a cleared space at the forest edge with a few carefully placed blocks of coral — a shrine of sorts. We found the caretaker and made a gift of cigarettes and a few coins. The caretaker took me to the beach, where he picked up damp sand and pressed it onto my cheeks and tied a tendril of green vine around my head as a garland. 'You now belong to the island,' he said.

These words thrilled me. So opposite, I thought, from a Western perspective where someone might be symbolically given the keys of a city, as if to say, 'The city belongs to you.' Here I belonged to the island. I-Kiribati have a phrase for this connection: tangiran abam, the love and longing they feel for their home islands.

When writing about rising seas and Pacific atolls it has struck me as ironic that the outside world is in a lather of alarm over the demise of islands while on the islands themselves time runs slow, people aren't in a hurry and the rhythms of life seem timeless, from the *switch, switch, switch* of a whisk broom at sunrise, sweeping up breadfruit leaves that have dropped in a yard overnight, to the sunset happy hour when women share a bowl of food while luxuriating in the lagoon.

When I was in Fongafale, I used to walk to the airfield in the late afternoons to watch daily games of volleyball and football on the runway and observe men balancing buckets of slops on their motorcycles to feed their pigs in ramshackle pens overlooking the sea.

One afternoon I saw a fisherman selling fresh tuna from a cooler box in front of his house, and stopped to buy some. He cut me a thick fillet, then refused to accept any money for it. When I admitted that I had no actual means of cooking the fish, he insisted I come into his home, and his wife cooked it while the fisherman showed me how he makes fibreglass tuna lures, using packets of fruit-juice crystals for colouring.

On another motor scooter ride through Fongafale, I was pleased to find Tuvalu's former governor-general sitting shirtless in the same breezy open-sided sleeping platform where I had met him 10 years earlier. His wife was resting next to him, using a piece of coral rock for a pillow.

We talked, and I reminded the elderly statesman of something he had told me during my last visit. It was a traditional saying, spoken to young people who leave their villages for the bright lights of foreign shores: 'Your climbing rope awaits you.' No matter how long you are away from Tuvalu, the islands will draw you back. Then you will take your place in the community, climbing the coconut palms once more.

The phrase has stuck with me. It makes me think of the resourcefulness, flexibility and perseverance of island life. You work with what you've got. You lose some, you win some — much like the reef islands themselves, abrading and accreting through geological time. You endure.

When Tevi Teaero wrote a series of poems addressing climate disruption he was going to call them 'Songs of Sinking Isles'. But that sounded defeatist, and didn't reflect his optimism about cultural renewal. So he called them 'Songs of Rising Isles'. One poem ends with these lines:

These isles of mine
Garlands of the gods
Will rise higher than tides
Forever ever more

I admire Tevi's hopefulness in the face of the seismic threats
that loom for atoll nations. The ancient name for the main
group of the Kiribati islands (not including outliers now under
Kiribati jurisdiction, such as the Line Islands and Rawaki
Phoenix Islands) was Tungaru. Some scholars find in this word
the meaning of 'people standing together in front of a breaking
wave'. Waves breaking over Pacific homelands is becoming
a common reality, and will become more common and more
damaging as seas rise and storms strengthen. But broaden the
gaze and it is all of us who stand in front of a swelling wave of
climate harm. It will be humanity's greatest test of endurance.

Cry, the
beloved ocean

ON CAPE TOWN'S WESTERN shoreline, near a big-wave surf spot called Dungeons, is a small, flat island that rises just a few metres above the surrounding sea. Duiker Island is more of a platform than an island — a haulout for several thousand Cape fur seals that have made it their own. They snooze and bellow and nurse their pups, and now and then heave themselves into the Atlantic, where snorkellers can join them in their frolics around rocks and through kelp forests. Sunlight sparkles on air bubbles trapped in their fur, and when they somersault and speed away, they trail a champagne wake.

Duiker Island lies within the Karbonkelberg Marine Reserve, a no-take sanctuary inside a much larger protected area that includes most of Cape Town's coastline. Karbonkelberg is the kind of place where a person, enchanted by whiskery seal faces and bulging seal eyes staring into their own, can feel that all is well in the watery world.

Unless, as I did, they were to look up and notice a line of men toiling up a hillside path with heavy sacks on their backs. Breaking away from the gymnastic seals, I swam to a tiny cove and stepped ashore onto a carpet of discarded abalone shells. They were the size of soup bowls, and they shimmered with nacreous shades of pink and green, like scenes from an aurora. The air was pungent with the stench of seals, dead molluscs and rotting kelp. An ibis stalked among the shells, pecking scraps of abalone guts. I climbed onto a flat-topped boulder that earlier in the day had been a shellfish abattoir. Here the men had thumbed the meat out of the shells and filled their sacks.

I followed the steep zigzag path up from the cove through fields of red and purple wildflowers to a ridge overlooking the township of Hangberg. This track is the 'poachers highway', along which hundreds of tonnes of illegal perlemoen are carried each year. The meat enters a supply chain of middlemen and processors, bound for Hong Kong and the East, where the shellfish is esteemed as a delicacy and an aphrodisiac.

In South Africa, abalone is a synonym for failure: of law enforcement, of fisheries management, and of the social contract that underpins sustainable use of the sea. Abalone is a collapsed fishery, and those who poach it are widely reviled as vultures enriching themselves from the last pickings of a dying resource.

But abalone is part of a much wider marine tragedy. Two-thirds of South Africa's commercially caught inshore finfish stocks, known as linefish, have crashed. In 2000 the government declared a state of emergency and slashed fishing effort by reducing the number of commercial licences. Yet many linefish stocks remain at perilously low levels — dead fish swimming. Commercial fishing of 40 traditionally important linefish species is prohibited. Even the national fish, a half-metre-long mussel-crunching bream known as the galjoen, is included in this ban.

New species are being added to the list all the time. In Struisbaai, near the southern tip of South Africa, I spotted a handwritten sign in the port office window: 'Red steenbras closed to all.' One of South Africa's premier game fish could no longer legally be caught.

The giant breams had been an angling institution. Up to 2 metres long and 70 kilograms in weight, capable of severing the fingers of the unwary, they were exciting to catch, delicious to eat and as plentiful as the stars in the southern sky. When they massed for spawning they turned the seas around Cape Town red. Now they were almost gone, and with the finality of the slam of a jailhouse door the government had decreed: 'Red steenbras closed to all.'

Here in five scribbled words was a disaster that not just South Africa but the world has belatedly woken up to: the oceans are being emptied of fish. The long sleep of denial is over. Ninety per cent of the world's fish stocks are either at maximum exploitation or on the downward slide to extinction. Today no sane person would say, as Charles Darwin's staunch supporter Thomas Huxley did, that 'the great sea fisheries are inexhaustible . . . nothing we do seriously affects the number of the fish'.

In fish-loving, fishing-mad South Africa, the anguish of declining catches and vanishing species has been acute. But if there's a crisis of fish, there's also a crisis of fishers. Half of South Africa's subsistence fishing communities are described as food insecure, because the foundation of their livelihood is in jeopardy. Yet in 1994, when Nelson Mandela was elected president of newly democratic South Africa, his African National Congress (ANC) party saw fish as a social equaliser and an uplifter of the impoverished. The rainbow nation would offer its marine resources as an egalitarian pot of gold for all.

Initially the prospects for social transformation looked good. Thousands of black and coloured South Africans, collectively known as 'historically disadvantaged individuals', obtained fishing rights. By 2004, more than 60 per cent of the commercial fishing quota was in the hands of this group, compared with less than 1 per cent 10 years earlier.

But as the linefish emergency showed, the government had invited more guests to the buffet than there was food to feed them. Even worse, an entire category of fisher had been left off the guest list. The new fisheries policy applied to commercial, recreational and subsistence fishers, the last group being those who fish only to eat, not to sell. Small-scale or artisanal fishers weren't included. They weren't considered subsistence fishers, because they sold their catch to make a living, but their trade was well below what could be considered commercial. More importantly, they thought of themselves as part of fishing communities, not as individual operators. They sought collective rights and communal access to resources, and they found themselves out of step with a quota system based on privatised ownership. For these small-scale operators, exclusion from the allocation process felt like a stinging reminder of apartheid.

There was an additional source of alienation, something that in a perfect world would be their best friend: marine protected areas, those fragments of coastal sea and seabed that are set aside for protection from human exploitation. Marine life flourishes within each blue oasis and spills over into neighbouring fishable seas, enhancing catches and sustaining livelihoods.

'MPAs function like a bank account,' marine biologist Bruce Mann told me at the Oceanographic Research Institute in Durban. 'You invest your money, and you have the security of knowing you've always got it there. But you also get some interest — a little bit of spillover you can live off.'

For many small-scale fishing communities, however, MPAs rub salt into the wounds of inequality — especially if a no-take area lies on the community's doorstep, as it does at Hangberg, where the Karbonkelberg sanctuary includes all the accessible shoreline for kilometres. The fishing community at Hangberg neither accepts the validity of the reserve nor respects the regulations associated with it.

It was this tug-of-war between environmental ambitions and social demands that had brought me back to South Africa, 12 years after I first wrote about these spectacular seas. Was it possible for South Africa to simultaneously preserve its marine life, maintain its fisheries and uplift its people? Or would there be more signs in port office windows about species that are 'closed to all'?

Hangberg sprawls across the side of a hill overlooking the Cape Town beach suburb of Hout Bay, a marginalised community living in marginal housing on the margins of the city. Above its rickety shacks and bungalows looms a crag called the Sentinel. The township has become a place of many sentinels. The poachers employ spotters, who watch out for police officers. Police informers are also watching, pimping on the poachers. A proud community has become a shadowland of crime, protest and defiance.

I walked through Hangberg's maze of alleys with Donovan

van der Heyden, a youth worker and community organiser — and a former poacher. Wetsuits hung on washing lines, and dope smoke drifted over the tin roofs. Donovan, his dreadlocks tucked under a Rastafarian cap, spoke of the community's long memory of dispossession.

'There's a lot of anger,' he said. 'The community looks back at how much the white fishing industry got from the resource and says, "Who's the poacher here? You had it. You messed it up. Now that we're claiming our share we are being blamed for depletion of the resource. But over how many years were you doing the same thing?"

'That's why I became a so-called poacher,' Donovan told me. 'It was my way of making a statement about injustice.'

The community's feeling of betrayal, he said, sprang from the fact that the government, in its eagerness to open fisheries to new entrants, sidelined bona fide fishers. 'Everyone jumped in — politicians, teachers, lawyers. People quit their professions to get into the industry because it was so open. And now they've got a grip, they're not letting go.'

We stopped beside a hole-in-the-wall convenience shop. Purple-leafed bougainvillea spilled over a razorwire fence, and Henry Adams, a swarthy 55-year-old with tattoos on his forearms, came to the gate to talk. For 17 years he had fished up and down the coasts of Africa. Here in his hometown, he can't survive on his legal permits. 'They gave quota to people who don't know the sea,' he said. 'So now I must poach. Quota made me illegal.'

Adams is not an abalone diver. He goes after crayfish — kreef. He rows miles in a night to catch them with small hoop nets. If police come, he hides in the sea bamboo where outboard motors can't follow. He has been caught and prosecuted four times. It makes no difference, he said. 'I will fish until my dying day, regardless of permits.'

A few streets away we came upon a sleek military-grey inflatable. Some young men were replacing the propellers on its two massive outboards. The boat's owner came out of a house. He told us his name was Joe and said he wasn't going to talk to us. To be a successful poacher, he said, you had to 'operate like a mouse, softly, quietly'. Then he spent the next 20 minutes denouncing the government's fisheries policy.

'I thought when the ANC came in to power they would take the white people's large quotas, chop them up into small pieces and give a piece to each fishing household just to survive,' Joe said. 'But what did they do? They played eeny meeny miny moe. If you didn't shout loud enough, you didn't get a quota. And to apply for a quota you have to be a rocket scientist. They make it so difficult.'

Fishing communities split into factions — bona fide fishers on one side, opportunists on the other. 'It was divide and rule,' said Donovan, himself a fourth-generation fisherman. 'The government fostered the individualistic approach, and as a result the resource suffered and the communities suffered.'

To fisheries managers, the perlemoen resource isn't just suffering, it's catatonic. Elsewhere in the Cape province, abalone stocks have crashed. It is only a matter of time before this coast's shellfish are decimated, they say.

The Hangberg fishers disagree. They say they rotate their fishing effort, letting harvested areas rest. There are a multitude of cracks and crannies in the rocks where abalones wedge themselves: de facto sanctuaries. Nor do they take undersized abalone, they say, because the Chinese market doesn't want them.

'And you must remember,' Joe said, 'that you can't go and poach every day. Sometimes there are storms, and for three weeks you must put a rock in the pot and make rock soup. We and Mother Nature, we protect the abalone.'

Beneath the swagger and the Robin Hood rationale, I detected doubt. Even ebullient Joe admitted, 'our bank is going bankrupt.' The community has seen what happened on the south coast, where the poachers poached themselves out of business. The Hangberg fishers say they're more responsible, but they're spinning the roulette wheel all the same, betting heavily on the resilience of the abalone population.

They may be misreading the odds. Marine conditions change in ways humans cannot reliably predict. In recent decades there has been an influx of crayfish into abalone areas. Crayfish eat the urchins that protect baby perlemoen under their spines. A boom in crayfish numbers could result in heavy losses to abalone populations. 'Mother Nature' might not protect the abalone in the numbers Hangberg fishers want.

Donovan told me he stopped poaching when he realised the amount of perlemoen being taken was jeopardising the future of the fishery. Others refuse to face the reality of depleted stocks, he said. He spoke bitterly about the arrogance and ignorance of the current poaching syndicates, which he estimated to number more than 250 people. 'It's no longer about livelihoods, it's about greed for a bloated, flashy lifestyle. These idiots can't see that the resource should be for their children and grandchildren.'

When I met him, Donovan was working as a part-time social worker, gardener and fibreglasser. 'It took me a while to address the moral issues,' he said. 'I realised I was part of the problem. As a poacher, I was enriching the people who were bringing drugs and crime into the community. If I got caught I would have failed the youth I'm trying to help.'

Donovan regretted that he had lost his connection to his Khoisan roots, to the strandlopers, coast walkers, whose lives as hunter-gatherers were intimately interwoven with the geography and ecology of place. He wanted to recover that sense of connection and identity.

He also worried about the kind of community Hangberg was becoming, defined by the so-called illegitimacy of some of its residents. The government needed to talk to the fishers not as 'children, idiots or criminals', he said, but as those whose lives depend on the sea and who have a legitimate claim to be consulted on its use and management.

Change was afoot. Communities had begun making the case that closed areas infringe on their constitutional right of access to food. That argument had gained legal and political traction, and pressure was mounting on the government to rezone some MPAs and open them to artisanal fishing.

That prospect appalled marine scientists I met. They urged — begged — the government not to open MPAs. If you open one, the rest will fall, they said. Fifty years of fisheries and conservation benefit would be wiped out in a matter of months. 'Raiding MPAs must be the stupidest option of all,' fisheries ecologist Colin Attwood told me. It was tantamount to robbing a bank, or spending your children's inheritance.

But it has happened. In 2016, South Africa's oldest marine reserve, at Tsitsikamma, between Plettenberg Bay and Cape St Francis, was partially opened to fishing by members of local communities. Some of South Africa's 40 other coastal MPAs may follow suit. There may be no other way to balance ecological objectives and human needs. As marine scientists themselves now acknowledge, the ecological dimensions of marine protected areas cannot be separated from their social and economic impacts, both positive and negative. Yet in the past, those impacts were rarely considered in MPA planning and management. The uncoupling of human and biological realities has led to frustration and anger, undermining conservation efforts.

I saw this for myself when I drove 120 kilometres north of Cape Town to meet subsistence fishers at Langebaan, a sinuous saltwater lagoon on South Africa's wave-pounded west coast. Langebaan's sheltered marshes, sandbars and turquoise-blue shallows are an important fish nursery and refuge, and a feeding habitat for hundreds of species of birds, from falcons to flamingos. The lagoon is also a traditional fishing ground for a small coloured community.

Oom (Uncle) Billie Smith took me out on the lagoon to fish for harders — the bread-and-butter fish of the west coast. Harders, or South African mullet, have been netted here since the 1600s. Most are salted and dried to make bokkoms — fish jerky. Oom Billie has fished for them all his life. In his younger days he also went after larger fare: sperm whales. Langebaan was a whaling station until the 1960s.

A small outboard powered Oom Billie's heavy open dinghy, or bakkie, across the lagoon to a sheltered spot where he paid out his net. It was a calm day, and he wasn't confident of much of a catch. He likes to fish when it's blowing upwards of 35 knots — conditions that keep recreational boats off the water and stir up the bottom, providing food for the fish.

The fishers work mostly at night, when they have the

lagoon to themselves. They fish without lights, to make it more difficult for seals to find them. Seals tear holes in their nets and can take a sizable portion of their catch. Fishers say the seals have more rights than they do. National park rangers, who enforce the MPA rules, say the fishers switch off their navigation lights so they can cross the line into the restricted zone undetected. The fishers don't deny it. Their working lives have become a cat-and-mouse game with the authorities.

After half an hour, Billie pulled the net in. We had three small harders. Cormorants had taken another two. As he had predicted, it wasn't much of a day for fishing. We puttered around the lagoon, and he named every rock, point, bay and reef we passed. I had heard it said that Langebaaners can navigate their lagoon blindfolded, and watching Billie I believed it. But their world has changed utterly. With a casino at one end and seaside mansions choking the cliffs at the other, Langebaan has become a resort, and the sea is a playground for the rich, not a workplace for the poor.

Oom Billie pointed to properties on the Langebaan shorefront that the community had owned before apartheid came. Then a line was drawn — whites to the south, coloureds to the north — and a community was upended. Now there are lines in the sea. In 1985, a national park and an associated MPA were created to protect wildlife above and below water. The lagoon was partitioned into three zones: an area adjacent to the town for fishing and recreation; a restricted zone where some white fishers are permitted to net commercially; and at the closed end of the lagoon, a no-take sanctuary where no boats are permitted.

The coloured fishers are only permitted to cast their nets in the recreational zone adjacent to the town, which they must share with up to 400 power boats and an armada of kiteboards and jetskis. 'We catch the schooling fish near the surface,' the fishers said. 'How can we do that when the boats drive through the fish schools, and through our nets? The fish go to the restricted zone, where we are not allowed.'

To the fishers, the MPA looks like another kind of forced removal. Not a symbol of promise — nature's bank, with interest payments for all — but a continuing sentence of exclusion and denial.

I joined a group of fishers at the home of Solene Smith, a community leader and chairperson of the Fishers of Langebaan. They were sheltering from the sun in a strip of shade behind the house, talking and passing a bottle. It was Sunday, drinking day. The firewater flowed, tears flowed, and anger flamed in the fishers' eyes and voices. One of them was about to face prosecution for fishing in the restricted zone. He would most likely have his boat confiscated. But this would not stop the fishers trespassing to catch mullet. They do not accept the legitimacy of the zoning divisions and they dispute the government's assessments of fish stocks. By the fishers' reckoning, they are not robbing the bank but exerting their rights not just as customers but as foundation shareholders.

What needles the fishers most is that, through a land-for-access deal struck at the time the national park was formed, three white families have permits to fish commercially in the restricted zone. Yet this was the Langebaaners' traditional fishing ground. Solene's husband, Edward, fixed me with his watery eyes. 'Tell me something,' he said. 'Why must you fish there, and I can't fish there? Because you're white? I want to fish there, too.'

Solene was wearing a sea-blue T-shirt with the slogan 'Unite and fight for fishers' rights'. Solidarity has emboldened the small-scale fishers, and recent legal victories have strengthened their arm. Courts have upheld the customary rights of traditional fishers and required that fisheries legislation be modified to allow a community-based approach to managing marine resources.

Many marine scientists consider these developments to be a backward step. 'Just as we're trying to reach conservation targets and create new protected areas, existing MPAs are being put on the chopping block,' Bruce Mann told me. He and others have been working on an MPA expansion strategy that aims to have 15 per cent of the country's total marine territory under no-take protection by 2028 — 'an ambitious goal for any maritime nation,' he said. A little over 5 per cent is currently protected. But if MPAs are reopened, that number will fall. To the scientists, it felt like trying to lay railway tracks while behind you people are tearing up the rails.

'We've tried very hard to reduce fishing effort on many of our species because we knew we were fishing them too hard,' he said. 'Now, with equity redress, we're putting pressure straight back on to those resources. Yes, people are hurting. They're hungry and need food. But these fishers will be harvesting what we've managed to claw back over four decades, and it's going to get flattened in a very short time. It's terribly complicated and emotional.' For scientists as well as fishers: the scientists feel sick at the thought of MPAs being opened, and the fishers feel sick at the thought of them staying closed.

Could cooperative fisheries management — the state working in partnership with the communities — thread the needle between ecological protection and social justice? A revised small-scale fisheries policy released by the government in 2012 claimed to be a paradigm shift in that direction: governance from the bottom up rather than imposed from the top down. The policy aims to give small-scale fishers the communal rights they crave, along with preferential access to marine resources. But will it resolve the issue of too many people wanting to fish?

The problem of oversubscription showed up starkly for me in the northeast of the country, in 275-kilometre-long iSimangaliso Wetland Park, one of South Africa's largest MPAs. At its northern end, near the Mozambique border, I waded into Kosi Bay estuary to meet Themba Mkhonto, who was working on his fish trap.

Fish trapping is a centuries-old practice at Kosi Bay, and Themba's trap had belonged to his father and grandfather before him. No bait is involved. The fish follow a brushwood palisade, curved like a hook, that guides them into one or more circular pens or kraals. They get into the kraal through a cunning arrangement of criss-crossed sticks; easy to enter, hard to exit. Once inside, large fish cannot escape, but small ones can squeeze through the gaps between stakes, which are tied with thick fibre stripped from the leaves of wild banana palms. Each day, the trap owner climbs into his kraals and spears any fish that have arrived during the night.

I asked Themba why he fished with a trap and not with a more efficient monofilament gillnet. With a trap, he said, you catch one fish, or two, or three every day. This is good. With a net you catch 10, 20, 50. This would be 'not good for me,' he said, including himself in the sustainability equation.

Themba's sense of self-limitation is no longer the norm.

The collapse of the migrant labour system at the end of apartheid brought a flood of workers back to their traditional lands on the coasts. Jobs were scarce, so they asked the local indunas, the sub-chiefs, what they should do. 'Build a trap,' the indunas said. 'Catch some fish.' Within six years the number of traps had doubled and the number of fish-collecting kraals had more than trebled. Today the estuary looks like a fish-trap maze, and you wonder how any fish at all can swim that gauntlet. There are even more traps upstream, in a string of four linked lakes.

Many of the newer traps have been built with nontraditional materials: straight eucalyptus and bamboo poles tied with nylon twine, instead of more irregular branches and thick banana-palm lashings. The modern traps have narrower gaps in the kraal walls that prevent undersize fish from escaping.

The real problem, however, isn't trap density and gap size, but changing attitudes, says Scotty Kyle, a fisheries scientist who has been studying the lake system and its idiosyncratic traps for 30 years. We were sitting outside his house, in a forest glade overlooking the largest of the Kosi lakes, having coffee and rusks — a standard South African breakfast.

'A subsistence fishery run by old men subsidising their pensions has become a youngster-driven commercial fishery using modern materials,' he explained. 'Some of these traps are big commercial concerns. The people running them have four-by-four vehicles and are exporting the fish out of the area.'

Of particular concern to Scotty was a new practice of building traps that face downstream. Traditionally, the palisades faced upstream, so as to catch fish only after they had matured in the lakes and were on their way back to the sea to spawn. 'Now the fish get smashed on the way out to the spawning grounds, and get smashed on the way back in,' he said. 'It's a double dip, and it's catching undersized fish.'

The average length of grunter, a fish in the sweetlips genus that is one of the main trap-caught species, has almost halved since Scotty began his work. In his view, the trade-off between the local community and the park authority — traditional access rights for a low-impact fishery — has been compromised. Or, to put it another way, there are not enough Thembas in the system.

Themba himself didn't know how this problem could be solved. Traditional authority structures struggle to contain aggressive self-interest. 'To control fishing is the right thing,' he said, 'but the government must talk to the people. The government must remember that the people suffer every time.'

My conversations with black and coloured communities invariably circled back to the legacy of suffering created by colonialism and apartheid. When iSimangaliso (the word means 'miracle' in Zulu) became a national park and, later, a World Heritage Site, Themba's people were told that they could no longer live by the sea. Their presence was inconsistent with the goals of nature preservation, so they were moved inland. To Themba, the displacement was illogical as well as unjust. His people have never accepted the Western notion of protected areas as conservation fortresses, with humans excluded.

He gave me an example. In earlier times, he said, hippos foraging around the lakes occasionally trampled the fences of the fish traps. Local people accepted this collateral damage as part of living with nature. 'The people stay here with the hippo. The people still alive. The hippo still alive. We stay together. Then the nature conservation come and say, "It is my hippo. You must go away from here."'

The people of eNkovukeni, a village perched on dunes between the Kosi lakes and the sea, refused to move. I walked there one morning with two boys I'd met in the nearby town of Manguzi. We followed a path through hippo grass, wading in water the colour of cognac, then crossed a ribbon of land between two lakes. I heard singing. Up ahead, a knot of people dressed in white stood at the water's edge for a baptism. Some of them held tall wooden crosses, and one lifted a burning candle aloft, Statue of Liberty-style. Their harmonies drifted across the water, evoking biblical times. A man of slight build with a rope cord around his shoulders and waist — the leader of this Zionist congregation — could have been John, baptising on the banks of the Jordan.

We stopped at the hut of a man named Titus, who took his fishing rod and led us across the dunes to the sea. Along the way we snacked on pale marula fruits and purple sea grapes, and the boys chased insouciant blue-and-yellow butterflies that danced from bush to bush. At the coast, Titus dropped to his hands and knees and dug in the coarse sand for ghost crabs to use as bait. He walked out on the black-rock reef, where the swells of the Indian Ocean were sending up curtains of spray. He stood a long time, squinting against the morning light, watching the curl of the green waves and the grey shapes of fish moving across their faces.

'I want them,' he said, and cast his line into the breakers.

They cast their souls, too, these people, to the mothering sea. They revere the sea. They even drink seawater to imbibe its curative essence. 'This is what we think,' Themba told me one evening as we sat under a shade tree with his family. 'If the sea stops, the people die. My father say, "Listen to me, my son. Do you want to know who is God? There he is."'

The people have a christening tradition that affirms their bond with the ocean. A newborn baby is taken down to the beach and placed on the wet sand. Just as a wave is about to wash over the infant, the mother rushes down and scoops it up. 'I have found my baby!' she exclaims. Presenting a child to the sea instils bravery as well as devotion, Themba said.

'Does this still happen today?' I asked. He replied: 'It happened to me.'

As winsome and enviable and necessary as that sense of connection is, the words of the Struisbaai port sign toll like a funeral bell. Spiritual bond or no spiritual bond, there will be no fish for tomorrow without protection today.

'We cannot do without no-take MPAs,' Bruce Mann said. 'They are our last resort.' They are not only ecological refuges and fish banks, they provide benchmarks and baselines. They reveal the default settings of the ocean. And they may be the last place to see species that have been harried to the point of extinction.

I learned there was a resident red steenbras at Castle Rocks marine reserve, beside the hook of land that is Cape Peninsula, so one morning I went there to look. I knelt on the seafloor while ocean swells swayed the kelp fronds and soft corals like an undersea wind. There were fish everywhere. I saw Cape knifejaw and galjoen flitting through the kelp canopy like birds in a rainforest. Broad-shouldered romans, brick-red with spatterings of white, muscled in close, and dainty French madames pecked at the bait I held, as if nibbling a madeleine.

A leopard catshark wriggled under a ledge inches away. I slipped my hands under it and lifted it out. It lay as straight and still as a baguette. I laid it back under the ledge and watched it scuffle away.

In an open area where waves had formed the shelly seabed into furrows, seven-gill sharks cruised slowly past, ghostly shapes in the misty water. Their eyesight is poor, which perhaps accounts for the fact that they passed just inches from my face. Who knows what they were processing with their battery of sense organs embedded in their blunt cartilaginous snouts. One glided beneath my outstretched hand. I felt its skin from its head to the twitching tip of its tail.

My dive partner pointed, and here came Castle Rocks' resident red steenbras, finning through the crowd. Red steenbras are now so rare that divers have given them names. This was Rupert, named after its species, *rupestris*. Though not one of the 2-metre monsters of yore, he was an impressive fish nonetheless, with the angular snout of a high-speed train, and his bronze-red flanks gleamed.

If people could just see this, I thought. If politicians and fisheries managers and fishers of every stripe could witness this abundance, they would understand how MPAs work and why it is in all their interests to safeguard them. Here begins the recovery from the sea's dying.

Connection
and protection

I HEAR THE TREES LAUGHING. On closer inspection, it is not the trees but angel terns — snow-white seabirds with black ink blots for eyes and a long blue-and-black thorn for a bill — which are producing prolonged, high-pitched cackles. The sound starts in their throat like a subdued chuckle, then they open their bills and out pours their hysterical chatter. D'Arros Island is waking to another Seychelles morning.

I hear the thud of a falling coconut in the palm forest and the soft crash of waves on the shore. A giant tortoise pauses in its grazing of the dewy grass to regard me, then takes a few steps and bends its wrinkled head to the sward once more. Giant tortoises move with the creaking sound of a leather saddle. They are land animals, but some have been known to take to the sea. One floated from Aldabra, in the western Seychelles, to Kenya. By the time it arrived its shell was covered in barnacles, like a turtle's.

I walk to the grass airstrip that bisects the island's palm forest. Frigatebirds are swirling high above the palms like black leaves. They are superb aerialists, with the highest ratio of wing area to body weight of any bird. They can climb to altitudes of more than 3 kilometres, sometimes making use of updraughts within cumulus clouds to boost their ascent, and they can stay aloft for weeks at a time.

From the southern end of the airstrip I look across a narrow channel to the atoll of St Joseph, an expanse of reefs, sand cays, islets and lagoon that is 10 times the size of D'Arros. Both islands are managed as nature reserves by the Save Our Seas Foundation (SOSF). I have come to these privately owned islands to see the foundation's work. The visit is part of my fieldwork for a story on conservation in the Seychelles for *National Geographic*.

When the tide drains from the lagoon, most of the reef flat at St Joseph dries and is worked over by millions of fiddler crabs. Being a violinist myself, I have an affection for these crustaceans with their one giant pincer, the fiddle, and their diminutive second pincer, the bow.

On the incoming tide, staff at the SOSF D'Arros Research Centre tell me, stingrays dig the crabs from their burrows. Shark pups and bonefish likewise come to the warm shallows to feed on shrimp and small fish. Full tide brings adult blacktip reef sharks and sicklefin lemon sharks in search of the smaller predators that have preceded them.

Hawksbill turtles feed on seagrass and shellfish in the silty shallows. As the tide recedes, some turtles move with it, while others hunker down in pools that reach human blood temperature in the tropical heat. This critically endangered species has been hunted since ancient times for its shell — the quintessential tortoiseshell of ornaments. The trade was outlawed in 2014, at which point only 20 per cent of the world's hawksbills remained. The D'Arros/St Joseph population is increasing, and is now one of the largest rookeries in the western Indian Ocean.

Hawksbills are studied by some of the staff at the research centre. So are sharks. I join Swiss doctoral student Ornella Weideli as she captures, tags and analyses sharks at St Joseph. She is studying how the juveniles of blacktip and lemon sharks partition habitat and food in order to avoid competition and coexist in a small, resource-limited lagoon.

She takes a blood sample from a four-month-old blacktip, the ninety-seventh shark she has tagged so far. She puts the blood in a test tube and I whizz it in a hand-cranked centrifuge. It's like winding a propeller. I count to 25 as the vials spin. When I've finished, the blood has separated into red cells and plasma. Ornella inserts a microchip into the pup and releases it. As we stand in the knee-deep lagoon we see a feathertail ray, shaped like a long-handled skillet, and a porcupine ray, pale and dappled like the sand, glide past.

Whenever I have visited or stayed at marine research stations — in Belize, Bimini, Great Barrier Reef, D'Arros — I have felt the exuberance and optimism of scientists and students as they work towards the goal of marine protection. D'Arros station science director Rainer von Brandis remarked that if marine science isn't put to use in marine conservation, 'what's the point?' He added: 'If I can help get marine protected areas established, I'll feel my work has meaning.'

In New Zealand, no one argued for marine protection more forcefully, or fought for it more doggedly, than Bill Ballantine, the first director of the University of Auckland's Leigh Marine Laboratory. Bill emigrated from England in 1964 to lead the marine lab, and lived at Goat Island for 50 years. When I was a marine biology student in the 1970s I used to see him kneeling on the rocky shore at low tide, measuring molluscs, putting his small measure of knowledge towards an understanding of the mystery of the sea.

Bill's speciality was limpets, and something of the limpet's legendary tenacity must have rubbed off on him. It took him 12 years to create the country's first no-take marine reserve at Goat Island. He spent another 40 trying to secure similar protection for other parts of New Zealand's coastline.

Bill believed New Zealand should be a leader in marine conservation. To him, it was a matter of simple geography. We are the most maritime nation on earth. We are at least 1500 kilometres from any other landmass. Our waters extend from the subantarctic to the subtropical, from the shallow continental shelf to the abyssal depths. 'Our marine environment is magnificent,' he wrote. 'It is not some trivial extra, like the ribbon on a parcel, but a major asset, worthy of our care and attention.' It made sense that we should lead the world in the creation of marine reserves. And it infuriated Bill that our progress was so glacially slow.

'Do you know your Bible?' Bill once asked me, then quoted a line from the prophet Isaiah: '"Precept upon precept, line upon line, here a little, there a little." That's the history of marine reserves, and it will continue to be so.'

I used to visit him at his home whenever I was writing about marine reserves. We would sit at his kitchen table, always strewn with academic papers, journals and articles he was working on. He would talk and smoke. I would listen and ask questions. When I asked him once about New Zealand's reputation as a pioneer in marine conservation, Bill replied sardonically, 'Yes, New Zealand was ahead for twenty-five years — in a race of arthritic tortoises. Not exactly a huge achievement.'

He likened the process of establishing marine reserves to a drunk trying to get a key in a lock. 'You have to be sober enough to be at the right door, holding the right key, but beyond that it's just persistence.'

Bill saw clearer than most what is now apparent to all — that the seas are sorely and sadly depleted of life. Fished ecosystems have lost so many of their original features that they are 'ghost ecosystems'. In scientific terms, marine reserves are a necessary experimental control — the unmanipulated part of the global experiment called fishing. They are a baseline. They show us what should, and could, be present. They are needed because if nothing is preemptively set aside, it becomes impossible to imagine the undamaged state.

It was a great loss to marine conservation when Bill died in 2015. The community hall in Leigh where his memorial service was held overflowed with people who, like me, came to acknowledge the country's most persistent and effective advocate for keeping a few parts of the sea free from interference and ecologically intact.

The walls of the hall were decorated with fish woven from green flax. Their eyes were the shells of Bill's beloved limpets. The fish bore tribute to Bill's legacy: 44 no-take marine reserves stretching from the subtropical Pacific to the subantarctic, ranging in size from 750,000 hectares in the Kermadec Islands (part of the much larger Kermadec Ocean Sanctuary, which remains in legislative limbo seven years after it was proposed) to a tiny 17-hectare educational reserve north of Haast, said to be the best place in the country to spot Hector's dolphins from the shore.

Scientists, academics and family members recalled the life of a brilliant, argumentative, visionary, impatient, supportive, romantic man with a boundless passion for science and an unquenchable devotion to marine protection. But perhaps the most astute comment came from someone who didn't speak at the service: one of Ballantine's six grandchildren. On being told his poppa had passed away, the boy had asked his father, 'Who will look after the snapper now?'

Who, indeed. Tempting as it is to think that the machinery of marine-reserve creation that Bill helped set in motion will proceed of its own accord to deliver ever larger swathes of ocean habitat free from human exploitation, history suggests that won't be the case. Committed, insistent, dedicated individuals will always be required.

One of the aspects of Bill's character that wasn't much dwelt on in his memorial service, but which I admired, was his moral clarity on the subject of conservation ethics. Marine reserves are often advocated on economic grounds such as improved fisheries yields and enhanced ecotourism opportunities. Bill understood those utilitarian arguments, but he never had much use for them — a point he made emphatically to me one morning as we sat at his kitchen table.

'I've always said that to do anything for money is stupid,' he said. 'You tell me anything real that is properly decided by money. You're going to get married and raise children. If anyone told you the cost of that, would it make any difference? I'd like to put these market forces people up on a stage and ask, "Are you married?" "Yes." "Did you get a bargain?" Whatever he says, his wife will kill him! "Are you making any money out of your children yet?" If yes, he'd be put in jail. If no, he doesn't believe his own theories. I don't pay much attention to economic arguments for marine protection because I don't pay much attention to economic arguments for having schools or getting married.'

In the early days of marine conservation, Bill said, he and his allies had to fend off the aesthetic argument: Is it beautiful enough to be preserved? They argued that marine protection was needed for all habitats and ecosystems, not just for spectacular locations. 'Now we have to fend off the economic argument,' he said. 'How much will it return?' Marine reserves — like children and grandparents — have economic value, but 'that's not how we conduct the argument'. Like Aldo Leopold, the American philosopher-naturalist, Bill considered that a rationale for conservation based primarily on economic self-interest is hopelessly lopsided.

Bill liked to cite the example of English landowner and naturalist Charles Waterton, who built a 3-metre-high wall around part of his estate in the 1820s and closed it to shooting. 'Everybody else closed their estates to *other* people shooting there, but not to shooting full stop,' Bill told me. 'Waterton was considered a lunatic. Not simply eccentric — mad. He said, "I just want them to be there — the wildfowl, the deer." And I'm saying that about fish now. And mangroves, and other sea creatures. Not "Is this piece of coastline a biodiversity hotspot?" "Will it be a fish nursery?" "Will it attract tourism?" I just want them to be there.'

The last scientific paper Bill published, in 2014, ended with these words: 'I may not live to see marine reserve systems generally in place round the world (I am 75), but I am confident my children will see it happen, and that my grandchildren will merely ask why such an obviously sensible idea took so long.'

One of the great ecological realisations of the past few decades has been that trees in a forest are not collections of separate individuals, but members of interconnected networks. Trees communicate with each other. They cooperate. They share resources. They form partnerships mediated by the fungi that interlace their roots, binding them into a literal 'wood-wide web'.

Some botanists now speak of forests as superorganisms, having properties that are greater than the sum of their individual parts. Author Richard Powers, who drew deeply on this new understanding in his novel *The Overstory*, remarked: 'Every sense we have that it's every individual for itself out there, a competition among ruthless individual forces, is completely laid waste to by this vision of massive interconnection.'

It turns out that the sea isn't much different. The interconnectedness of marine life is broader and deeper than was ever suspected. One surprise has been the role that top predators such as sharks play in maintaining the health of tropical ecosystems, particularly coral reefs. On pristine reefs — those few remaining coral assemblages undamaged by fishing, pollution and other human disturbances — researchers have found that such predators account for most of the biomass of fish in the ecosystem. This unexpected discovery overturns the usual concept of a biomass pyramid, where primary producers (photosynthesisers) make up the largest component of biomass, forming the base of the pyramid, and various tiers of consumers make up the rest of the pyramid, with a few top predators at the apex. On pristine reefs the pyramid is flipped.

I wrote about the phenomenon in 2008 for *National Geographic* in a story about Kingman Reef, one of the most remote and pristine coral reefs in the world. Kingman Reef is the northernmost of the Line Islands, a chain of 11 islands and reefs that straddle the equator (the 'Line') between Hawai'i and French Polynesia.

Kingman's 40-kilometre triangle of coral reef encloses a lagoon the size of Lake Tarawera. Above water, nothing grows. The only dry land consists of a few spits of sun-whitened coral rubble and the broken shells of giant clams. But beneath the surface is a world of rare luxuriance. The reef is a rainbow city of staghorn, mushroom, pillar and plate corals packed so tightly there is hardly a patch of bare substrate. Through their interstices dart fusiliers and damselfish, butterflyfish and parrotfish, and scores more of the plankton sippers, coral nibblers and algae grazers that populate a reef-fish community.

Patrolling above the skyline of the coral city are the reef's overlords: grey and white-tipped reef sharks and hordes of aggressive red snapper. Fully 85 per cent of Kingman's fish biomass is in the form of these large predators, and three-quarters of the predator biomass is sharks — the opposite of the conventional image of a coral reef: throngs of aquarium-size fishes flitting through a coral garden, and barely a predator in sight. Kingman's proportion of apex predators is greater than has been found in any other coral reef ecosystem.

The significance of the reverse biomass pyramid, as it is known by reef biologists such as Enric Sala, who headed *National Geographic*'s Pristine Seas project and led the research at Kingman Reef, is that it provides a baseline for what a healthy reef should look like. Enric estimates that only a couple of dozen such reefs still exist on the planet. Places like Kingman Reef are rare exceptions to the rule of fished-out, ecologically unbalanced reefs. They have high coral density, very little algal growth, and low concentrations of disease-causing microbes. Reefs that experience high fishing pressure have the opposite.

Although the ecological mechanisms are not fully understood, it seems that the role of top predators is to keep mid-range predators in check, allowing herbivorous fish and urchins to flourish and keep algal growth to a minimum. Algae are a problem for coral reefs. If they get a foothold, they block the settlement of juvenile corals and increase the concentration of dissolved carbon in the surrounding seawater, boosting the growth of harmful bacteria and viruses that infect corals and can lead to their death.

Microbiologists on the research expedition found 10 times as many microbes in the water column above the algae-ridden reefs of nearby Kiritimati (Christmas Island), with a population of 2000 people and an almost complete absence of predators on its reefs, as they did at Kingman.

But Kingman's pristine state could easily be lost, Enric told me when I discussed the Kingman research with him, and ecological disaster is only an opportunistic fishing boat away. It would take just a few weeks for shark-finners to strip the reefs of sharks. Instantly, the health of the marine ecosystem would plummet. Without top predators, mid-range predator numbers would swell, herbivore numbers would tumble, and the resulting trophic cascade would allow algae to overtake the coral.

To Enric, the message of Kingman Reef is clear: 'Overfishing is ecological sabotage. It removes entire trophic levels. That's like removing vital parts from a machine and expecting it to keep functioning.' At Kingman, the machine still has all its parts. And because its ecological linkages are intact, it is a stable and resilient system, able to recover from environmental stresses such as marine heatwaves and coral bleaching. Kingman Reef provides a glimpse of what a coral reef should be.

A postcard from the past, it offers a pathway for reef recovery. But will its message be heeded?

I wrote about another example of ecological interconnection in a *National Geographic* story about two islands in the Mozambique Channel, between Africa and Madagascar: Bassas da India and Europa. They are the southernmost of Les Îles Éparses, the Scattered Islands, six specks of land that ring Madagascar like moons. Remnants of the once mighty French colonial empire, they fly the tricolore as part of France's Southern and Antarctic Lands. As with Kingman Reef, I wrote about this research without the benefit of visiting the islands themselves.

Europa is a tree-covered island where turtles nest and a million pairs of seabirds breed. Bassas da India is an atoll that, like Kingman Reef, barely shows above the waterline, with an 80-square-kilometre shark-filled lagoon. Both are among the last vestiges of healthy marine ecosystems in the western Indian Ocean — sanctuaries for wild nature in depleted seas.

'On the surface, they look like nothing — like insignificant dots,' photographer Thomas Peschak told me. 'But once you've dived here, you're spoiled for the rest of your life. Other places I go in the Indian Ocean now, all I see is what's missing.'

The southward flow of water through the Mozambique Channel — which eventually becomes the Agulhas Current that bathes the eastern coastline of South Africa — gives the appearance of a permanent and uniform stream, but oceanographers have found it to be a zone of meandering currents, thermoclines, sea-level variations and nutrient upwellings. It is a complex marine patchwork, with marine life scattered unpredictably through it. Areas of enrichment can appear and disappear with the seasons or in response to short-term weather shifts.

Because of the ecological linkage between seabirds and aquatic creatures, scientists can study this environment without even going to sea. They use birds as proxies for difficult-to-study marine predators such as tuna and dolphins. Many seabirds rely on these ocean-roaming hunters to drive smaller fish and invertebrate prey to the surface, within reach of their bills and talons. Such birds are now thought of as full-fledged marine organisms. They depend entirely on the sea for their sustenance; they just happen to live above it, rather than in it. Their foraging behaviour provides a window to the deep.

Some species, such as boobies and terns, form low-flying flocks that track marine life from just above the surface. Known as network foragers, they fan out from their roosts on land, keeping each other in sight, ever alert in case one should encounter prey. Other birds track the trackers, soaring to high altitudes to survey the panorama.

Frigatebirds are supreme among these high fliers. Two species breed on Europa: the great and the lesser frigatebird. They belong to the family Exocetidae. The Exocet missile was named after them — a fitting tribute to exceptional aerialists.

Great frigatebirds use thermals to rise to high altitudes, from where they scan not just the sea for prey but the horizon for other seabirds. When they spot a feeding flock, they swoop down on their black, angular wings — 2 metres from tip to tip — to join the feast, snatching squid from the waves or taking flying fish in midair. They work their deeply forked tails like scissor blades as they chase prey or engage in dogfights with other birds, often forcing them to drop or spew up their catch. Folk names for frigatebirds — man-o-war birds and scissors of the sea — evoke these high-speed aerobatics.

Soon the banquet is over. The tuna move on, their prey

disperse, and the patient flights of the foragers, crossing seas of unpredictability, continue.

The ecological links between fish and birds extend beyond the marine environment. Through seabirds' guano, fish fertilise the land. The land reciprocates, leaching nutrients back into the sea. This two-way nutrient subsidy is especially important for ecosystems that are nutrient poor. Coral reefs are such ecosystems. Scientists have found that fringing reefs near seabird colonies are enriched by nutrients flowing into the sea. In one study in the Gulf of California, corals close to a seabird colony were found to grow four times faster than those at more distant sites.

Overfishing breaks this linkage. A decline in large predatory fish means fewer surface concentrations of krill, squid and small schooling fish that are the primary food of diving seabirds. Seabirds go hungry, they lay fewer eggs, raise fewer chicks and deposit less guano on land. Soil fertility declines. Insects, lizards and other terrestrial animals have less to feed on. An entire land-based food chain is disrupted.

The longer I spend in and on the ocean, the more the boundary blurs between land and sea, fish and birds, water and air. In the Seychelles I watched flying fish launch themselves on gossamer fins and glide dozens of metres, staying aloft for a breathtaking 30 seconds or more before splashing down, and then, moments later, soaring again.

If flying fish seem to want to be birds, then a multitude of petrels, shearwaters, shags, gannets and albatross, dipping and plunging beneath the waves, seem to want to be fish. Penguins have become semi-permanent residents of the sea. Some are truly pelagic, returning to land only to moult and breed. Others spend their days at sea, returning in the evening to land. Emperor penguins, pushing the definition of bird, can dive to 500 metres and stay underwater for up to 30 minutes.

In his documentary *Albatross*, photographer and filmmaker Chris Jordan makes the statement that every molecule of an albatross's body comes from the sea. 'There is no boundary between the albatross and the ocean,' he says.

That lack of boundary is both beautiful and terrible. As the seas have become filled with plastic, seabirds' bellies have become filled with a toxic slew of indigestible debris. As Jordan, who narrates the film, expresses it, 'They cannot know what plastic is. Their instinct is to trust what the sea provides.'

Trust has led to betrayal. Jordan takes the viewer to Kuaihelani Midway Atoll, in the Hawaiian archipelago, to witness the lives and deaths of the Laysan albatross that nest there. The movie's heartbreak lies in its documentation of the deadly toll of ocean-borne plastic on these ocean-spanning birds. We look over Jordan's shoulder as, dead bird after dead bird, he photographs their stomach contents: kaleidoscopes of fatal fragments that they have mistaken for food. The mingling of plastic and feathers in image after image is traumatic to view: feathers, so evocative of tenderness and comfort, interspersed with the jagged-edged discards of death.

Jordan is an artist, not a biologist, and he came to this project in an indirect way. It was an interest in photographing garbage, industrial junk and the detritus of mass consumption that first brought him to Midway. He followed the plastic trail from the cities of North America to its tragic terminus: the bellies of seabirds. And then he found he couldn't look away.

The documentary opens with an enigmatic line from

Samuel Taylor Coleridge's 'The Rime of the Ancient Mariner', the poem that fixed the albatross in the Western mind: 'He loved the bird that loved the man who shot him with his bow.' With those words Coleridge wove a living thread connecting human to bird to ocean.

The mariner severs the connection by killing the albatross. So have we. In the poem, the mariner kills his albatross instantly with a crossbow. We kill them slowly with our trash — and with fishing gear. Twenty-one of the 22 species of albatross are classified as vulnerable, threatened or endangered. Two are on the brink of extinction. Albatross are the most threatened family of birds in the world. Misfortune follows the mariner's act, and his fellow crewmen turn against him. 'Ah wretch! said they, the bird to slay.' The bird slayer is condemned to wear the albatross around his neck to mark his guilt.

But that's not the end of the story. For as much as the poem is about a curse, it is about a cure as well. The mariner awakens from his sleep of ignorance and separation. He praises nature's beauty and acknowledges the common bond between humans and their fellow creatures. 'A spring of love gushed from my heart, and I blessed them unaware,' says the mariner — and the curse is broken.

Jordan's film tracks his own journey from detached observer to grieving participant. 'I didn't know I could care about an albatross,' he admits. His meditation on grief is both poignant and hope-filled. 'Grief is the same as love. When we surrender to grief it carries us home to our deepest connection to life.'

From that connection comes the impulse to protect what needs protecting and to confront what needs confronting: a fishing industry with a vast and destructive ecological wake; a consumer economy that is profligate with its waste. In these unprecedented times for life on earth, it has never been more necessary to do this work of protection and confrontation on behalf of the oceans.

Understanding our connectedness is the first step — one that novelist John Steinbeck wrote about 70 years ago in *The Log from the Sea of Cortez*. The book recounts a six-week collecting trip through the Gulf of California (more colourfully known as the Sea of Cortez) that Steinbeck made with marine biologist Ed Ricketts, to whom Steinbeck dedicated his novel *Cannery Row*.

Midway through the log, Steinbeck muses on the central importance of ecological thinking, of seeing the inseparable whole. 'It is a strange thing that most of the feeling we call religious . . . is really the understanding and the attempt to say that man is related to the whole thing, related inextricably to all reality, known and unknowable. This is a simple thing to say, but the profound feeling of it made a Jesus, a St. Augustine, a St. Francis, a Roger Bacon, a Charles Darwin, and an Einstein. Each of them in his own tempo and with his own voice discovered and reaffirmed with astonishment the knowledge that all things are one thing and that one thing is all things — plankton, a shimmering phosphorescence on the sea and the spinning planets and an expanding universe, all bound together by the elastic string of time.'

To achieve such an understanding is as simple as kneeling beside a tide pool, something Steinbeck would have done hundreds of times during the voyage. All one has to do is 'look from the tide pool to the stars and then back to the tide pool again', he writes. If a person can do that, they will find the pool stretches two ways: in one direction to electrons and in the other to the universe. 'Then ecology has a synonym which is ALL.'

An ethic
for the sea

I WAKE TO THE SOUND of faint crackling, like electrical static. It seems to be coming from under the hull of *Marline*, which is anchored in Deep Water Cove, in the Bay of Islands. It is a calm, warm summer morning. The cove, flanked by the hills of Cape Brett peninsula, lies in shadow, but sunlight is flaring the craggy branches of pōhutukawa on the ridges.

The clicking is incessant, and I want to know what's causing it. I rouse myself to go on deck and look over the side, and the mystery is solved. Schools of fish are nibbling at the creatures that have attached themselves to the hull. It is the sound of their tiny teeth pecking at barnacle, bryozoan, alga and tubeworm that has woken me. I feel oddly pleased, as if I, a guest, am providing a breakfast snack for these residents of the bay.

More fish are shoaling near the kelp-fringed walls of the cove a dozen metres away. I watch them move for a few minutes in one direction, then turn as one and move back in the other. Soon I will slip into the water to join them.

This cove has become the best place to snorkel in the Bay of Islands, but it wasn't always so. When I was a teenager, this area was as ecologically depleted as anywhere in the bay. I would see ubiquitous parore, the occasional wary red moki, perhaps the turquoise flash of a fleeing snapper. Reefs were typically denuded of kelp and covered with grazing sea urchins.

In 2010, dismayed by the disappearance of marine life, two of the local hapū placed a traditional rāhui — a temporary fishing closure — on Deep Water Cove and the wider Maunganui Bay. Fishing was banned until stocks recovered. The rāhui has stayed in place, renewed every two years, and the results have been stunning.

Near the entrance to the cove, close to where the navy frigate *Canterbury* was scuttled as a dive attraction in 2007, is a shallow reef known to locals as White Reef. According to friends who have offered to take my partner and me snorkelling there, the reef was given that name because it was largely bare white rock with minimal algae and encrusting life. It was like much of the rocky coastline of New Zealand: a marine ecosystem profoundly out of balance through unsustainable fishing pressure.

The direct agent of algal depletion on rocky reefs is the humble kina, an endemic sea urchin. Kina are seaweed eaters, capable of felling even mature kelp by gnawing through their trunks. Kina in turn are preyed on by lobsters and snapper, which are favourite targets of fishers and divers. When lobsters and snapper become scarce through overfishing, kina numbers skyrocket, decimating the reef's algal community. The process is known as a trophic cascade and the result is called a kina barren. Think of it as underwater deforestation: forests of kelp felled by urchin loggers.

Removal of fishing pressure reverses the process. I remember diving at Goat Island in the late 1970s, soon after it became a no-take marine reserve. Kina barrens were characteristic of the bay, the result of decades of overfishing. But over successive years, as snapper and lobster numbers increased rapidly in the reserve, the kelp came back.

At White Reef the same thing has happened. White Reef should now be called Golden Reef, because it is covered in the waving gold, mustard and brown blades of a variety of kelps and other seaweeds. Through the underwater forest swim demoiselles, scarlet pigfish, black angelfish, striped red moki, snapper, eagle rays and pigment-daubed Sandagers wrasse, patterned like a Kandinsky painting. Above the forest float dozens of comb jellyfish, translucent oval animals that show flecks of jewelled colour when they catch the sunlight. I watch four leatherjackets, a type of triggerfish, peck at one jellyfish, reducing the frail creature to strands of jelly. Yellow-tailed kingfish patrol the perimeter, occasionally darting into the kelp to hunt bait fish.

It is a reef restored, and I am elated. It is the same feeling I have when I step ashore on a predator-free island sanctuary: exultant, awed, hushed. One such sanctuary is Moturua, an hour by launch from Deep Water Cove, one of several islands in the bay that have been freed from introduced predators in a campaign led by conservation group Project Island Song. Here I see birds I rarely encounter on the mainland. Tīeke, glossy black songbirds with a rust-red saddle, hop and flit through the forest, uttering a gloriously noisy call that sounds like an engine being cranked. Pōpokotea, or whiteheads, squeak in tall mānuka. A toutouwai, the North Island robin, cocks its head inquisitively, standing on the path on matchstick legs, then darts into the leaf litter to peck for grubs. I sit beside a pool where water trickles in and then tumbles over an escarpment, and watch miromiro and pīwakawaka — tomtits and fantails — bathe, dipping their bills and wetting their feathers. At night I see a juvenile kiwi, not much bigger than a rockmelon, striding across the forest floor on its stout legs, and hear the *scritch, scritch* stridulation of giant wētā.

In places like Moturua and White Reef I have the sense of being formed. Not informed — which has been a major motivation of my editing and writing life — but actually having my existence shaped by place. Land's identity-shaping agency is something I have seen and learned from my encounters with Māori. I remember my astonishment at discovering that in te reo Māori the words for land and placenta are the same: whenua. The nurturing land and the nurturing mother's body: one interconnected reality, one blood.

Māori kinship with land and water is nowhere expressed more succinctly than in the defining utterance of the tribes of the Whanganui River: 'Ko au te awa, ko te awa ko au.' 'I am the river, the river is me.' Yet I once heard a kaumatua say that Māori as a people did not exist prior to their encounter with Aotearoa a mere 700 or so years ago. They became tangata whenua, people of the land, through engagement with the land. 'We came here as Polynesian,' the elder remarked. 'The land made us Māori.'

Is this process of engagement leading to identity something that Pākehā (non-Māori) can experience, and an outcome to which they can aspire? To be inscribed into the fabric of the land, even as the land is inscribed in them? When writing about the Whanganui River for *National Geographic* in 2019, I put this question to Whanganui iwi leader Gerrard Albert. Could Pākehā experience a level of identification with land and water that would enable them to say: 'I am the river, the river is me'?

'That's what we want them to be able to say,' Gerrard told me. 'The river isn't just iwi, it's community — and that includes Pākehā communities. Let everyone acknowledge the kawa [customs and traditions] of the river. Kawa doesn't distinguish between Māori and Pākehā. Let everyone come in to that way of thinking.'

Tāmati Kruger, a leader of the Tūhoe iwi, which has custodianship of the forests of Te Urewera, told me something similar. 'I see a time when all of us, regardless of heritage, come to understand that in Aotearoa we are all tangata whenua. And that means that we are of this land, that this land has made us who we are. We have let this land create us in its image, and together we are proud of who we are and where we come from. In such a world we don't need a treaty or policy or laws to tell us what we must do. Kinship is our motivation, our kinship connection with the land. The Tūhoe view is that other people can love Te Urewera as much as Tūhoe people do. That as human beings, if we come to believe and adopt as our tradition that we come from nature, that nature creates us in its image, then that can become our identity.'

I find these generous words deeply heartening. They encourage me to follow my own pathway of kinship and connection, knowing a place like Moturua or White Reef in all its dimensions, animate and inanimate, and letting the place know me. Māori express this idea of reciprocity with the phrase 'Titiro atu, titiro mai' — one glance directed at another, the other glancing back. The world beckons, I respond. I see, and I am seen. I love a place, and am loved and nurtured by it in return. This idea of mutual care permeates all indigenous cultures. It is the equivalent of hongi, the pressing of noses, the essential Māori greeting: a sharing of the breath of life.

Melbourne ecophilospher Freya Mathews writes movingly of the path of becoming native to place. 'To belong to the land is to uncover its layers, discover its story, and weave one's own identity into that story,' she writes. 'Through a particular place, [the world] agrees to become our world, attentive to us, attuned to us. We become its people.'

I came to know Freya's writing during a voyage to Antarctica. It was a memorable voyage. I had her book *Reinhabiting Reality* on a desk that I was gripping with both hands against the rolling of the ship, 30 degrees one way, 30 degrees the other, with the regularity of a metronome. I was feeling simultaneously nauseous from the ship's motion and euphoric from what I was reading.

The reinhabiting Freya writes about is an invitation to reject a materialist way of thinking about the world and awaken to its communicative presence. To do so is to undergo a personal 'nativity' — one's own incarnation into the place of one's being. 'To be native is to have one's identity shaped by the place to which one belongs,' Freya writes. 'One is a creature of its topography, its colours and textures, saps and juices, its moods, its ghosts and stories. To be native is to experience the world as fundamentally continuous with one's own nature, rather than as an alien and lower realm of sheer mindless externality.'

This is precisely the experience of indigenous people. It often strikes me as ironic and sad that with all the afflictions the planet is now facing — biodiversity in steep decline, a climate in disarray, ecosystems teetering on collapse — that so few seek survival advice from the earth's longest continuously existing cultures, including, in Australia's case, groups who have occupied that continent for more than 50,000 years, and whose understanding of the interpenetration of people and place is at a level that boggles the Western mind.

For indigenous Australians, all the components of their place — their 'country' — are kin. They experience the world as 'a multitude of invisible threads of connection', writes anthropologist John Bradley, and engage with the matrix of that world in song. As they sing, 'country in all its wealth and vitality opens up in the singers' minds . . . They are seeing the land anew as it once was and they hope it will always be. A distillation of the power and sentience of the country is being revealed once more.'

The singing of country, which includes both land and sea, is a way of understanding its nature and adapting to its needs, so that, in turn, land and sea will meet their needs, says Bradley. For the Yanyuwa people of the Gulf of Carpentaria, this singing, known as kujika, 'is about love and the lifting up of space and place, of the only home that people have ever known'. It is the foundation of Yanyuwa identity and the expression of an ethic of care. As one Yanyuwa elder described it during a land claim meeting, 'Kujika holds us as one. It is the most important thing for us. White people do not know this. They have no ears to hear the country. But for us Yanyuwa speakers it is the Law. The kujika is the road in the country that we follow with a single intensity. It is for us and it holds us tight.'

Can Westerners develop ears to hear country — land country, sea country? I believe so. Developing kinship with the world around us, animate and inanimate, is a journey on which we can — and, for the sake of the future, must — embark. Though, in fact, in the Aboriginal world nothing is inanimate. The land has its own intelligence. Kujika animates all.

The path to kinship is also a path to custodianship. The

two are like breathing in and breathing out. We breathe in connection and identity and breathe out custodial care. And the very act of caring for country deepens the sense of connection. It is a circle of belonging.

For Māori, the kinship–custodianship bond is known as kaitiakitanga. A flourishing life is impossible without it. The Waitangi Tribunal made this point emphatically in a landmark report on Māori traditional knowledge. 'If hapū are unable to exercise their kaitiaki obligations, they are deprived of a core aspect of their culture,' wrote the report's lead author. 'Without kaitiakitanga, Māori are themselves lost.'

Aboriginal scholar Mary Graham explains that the custodial ethic is essential 'not only to Aboriginal society but to any society that intends to continue for millennia and wants to regard itself as mature.' That ethic, which is central to the Aboriginal term 'Law', is valid for all people, she writes, and can be acted on by anyone who is interested in caring for land and sea. Custodianship is a philosophy, not just an environmental action.

O ne of the challenges in developing a custodial ethic towards the sea is that oceans tend to be seen as undifferentiated expanses — spaces more than places. On land, protection and custodial care for the natural environment have coincided with a growing sense of place — appreciation of the particulars of places and a feeling of belonging. Mountains, waterfalls, crags, creeks, ponds, wetlands — all the manifestations of geology and geography combine to create landscapes that imprint on the mind. Place and person become joined in a bond of care.

Can the same process happen with the sea? For those who are intimate with the sea, similar geographies of place are present in the form of rocks and reefs, tides and eddies, shallows and depths, waves and whirlpools. Such features are nodes in a geographical matrix that creates a particular mind map. Māori know the sea with this intimacy. They named these places, gave them taniwha, wrapped them in story.

Places, writes British geographer Tim Cresswell, are a way of seeing, knowing and understanding the world. Seeing the world as places, not spaces, can be an act of resistance against the commodification of the world, he writes. 'To think of an area of the world as a rich and complicated interplay of people and the environment — as a place — is to free us from thinking of it as facts and figures.'

Epeli Hau'ofa lamented the commodification of the oceans that followed the signing of the United Nations Convention on the Law of the Sea, and especially its declaration of exclusive economic zones. The intention was good — to reduce international conflicts over fishing, mining, fossil fuel drilling and other forms of exploitation — but the effect was to compartmentalise the sea as property and resource, with a focus on its economic use and strategic importance rather than its deeper human values and associations. The convention fostered an inward-focused nationalism, not an outward-focused sense of community.

'It is one of the great ironies of the Law of the Sea Convention, which enlarged our national boundaries, that it also extended the territorial instinct to where there was none before,' wrote Hau'ofa in his essay 'The Ocean In Us'. 'Territoriality is probably the strongest spur for some of the most brutal acts of aggression, and because of the resource potentials of the open sea and the ocean-bed, the water that has united subregions of Oceania in the past may become a major divisive factor in the future relationships between our countries. It is therefore essential that we ground any new regional identity in a belief in the common heritage of the sea.'

A belief in common heritage is hard to achieve in societies that prioritise the rights and interests of individuals over the collective good. Earth's atmosphere is humanity's common heritage, but that knowledge has been a weak motivator of collective action. The 'commons' is today more often a place of tragedy than of triumph. Western societies have shifted away from the values of a shared heritage. We must look to indigenous cultures for an example of how to approach land, sea and air differently.

We could consider the relationship of Native American nations with salmon. In their worldview, salmon are kin, a neighbouring tribe, a people, a nation. It is said that salmon and humans spoke the same language, that they could take each other's form. In her book *Braiding Sweetgrass*, Robin Wall Kimmerer writes of the traditional ceremony of welcome by Pacific Northwest tribes to salmon making their pilgrimage to the rivers where their lives began. Fires were lit on the coastal headlands. The people gathered on the riverbanks to sing the salmon home and dance for their homecoming. The bones of the first salmon caught were placed back in the river as a symbol of renewal and the people's commitment to reciprocal care.

But industrial overfishing decimated the salmon population, the draining of wetlands robbed the fish of estuarine transition zones between salt- and freshwater, and the subjugation of the people dissipated the ceremonial knowledge. Kimmerer tries to fathom the loss and find hope for restoration of the relationship between fish and people. Her experience is the combination of emotions that many today feel: 'Joy for the being of the shimmering world and grief for what we have lost.'

Restoring a lost relationship with the shimmering world is possible. I think of the recent legislation that recognises Te Urewera forest and the Whanganui River as persons in law. This legislation points us in the direction of relationship with place and away from a commodified view of land and water as resources, controlled in New Zealand by the Resource Management Act — an Act whose very name enshrines a resource-centred attitude.

I recall what Gerrard Albert told me when I wrote about Te Awa Tupua, the river of sacred power. 'The Resource Management Act talks about a river defined by statutes, a river someone else has created, not the river that completes me. Te Awa Tupua is the river I recognise, the river I know. Our approach has been to claw back that river, and the new legislation allows for a paradigm shift to do that.'

We need that same paradigm shift for the sea.

From a nail on a bookcase next to where I have written this book hangs a tress of kelp dried and knotted by Northland weaver Toi Te Rito Maihi. I hang it here to remind me of an Inuit story I want to keep prominent in my mind, because it contains a message I must not forget. It is the story of the mother of the sea. The story is told with many variations across the polar north, and the mother herself has multiple names, including Sedna, Nuliajuk and, in Greenland, Sassuma Arnaa.

It is the Greenland version I am most familiar with. When

I was voyaging around southern Greenland in 2022 I saw the central motif of the story rendered in solid granite standing on the foreshore of the capital, Nuuk, and painted on murals in coastal villages dotted around the Greenland coast.

It was 10 years ago that I first heard of the mother of the sea, a creator and guardian of the ocean realm. The version I offer here is based on one told by David Pelly in his book *The Sacred Hunt*.

Long ago, there lived in the Arctic a beautiful young woman. Many men were presented to her as prospective husbands, but she rejected them all, until one day a handsome stranger came to her family's camp. He had many dogs and finely crafted hunting tools, and he promised her a life of comfort. She could not resist his charms, and she left with him for his land across the sea, only to find on her arrival that she had been deceived. Her betrothed was, in fact, a seabird who had taken human form, and his dwelling was a hovel.

Hearing of the deception, her father came to rescue her, and the pair escaped in his boat across a calm sea. But her seabird husband's spirit pursued them and whipped the icy sea into a raging storm. In mid-ocean in a small boat, the father feared for his life and, to appease the bird, cast his daughter overboard into the wave-tossed waters. But she clung tenaciously to the gunwale of his boat.

Determined to release her grip, the father cut off her fingers at the first knuckle. The pieces fell into the sea and became ringed seals. Still she held on. Then he cut her fingers at the second joint, and those pieces swam away as bearded seals. Other pieces of her fingers became walruses and whales. This is how the sea mammals were created, and that young woman became Sassuma Arnaa, the mother of the sea. To this day she lives at the bottom of the sea and controls all the animals in her watery domain.

Hunting success among the Inuit people depends on the benevolence of the mother of the sea. In normal times, when people are respectful of the natural world and in harmony with each other, she releases the animals to be hunted. But if humans fail to respect the natural world, neglecting the customs of honour towards the animals they hunt, she recalls the animals to live with her, and times become lean for the hunters and their communities.

The Inuit say that Sassuma Arnaa loves to have her hair clean and neat. Human transgression figuratively defiles and tangles her hair, filling it with knots. But she has no fingers with which to comb it, so a shaman is summoned. He prepares himself spiritually and dives through a hole in the ice and swims down to the dwelling of the mother of the sea. And what does he do when he gets there? He combs her hair, and in her pleasure at this demonstration of tender care she releases the animals to the hunters once again.

The intimacy of the shaman's action moves me, and recalls for me my first dives in the kelp forests of Tāwharanui when, like Cousteau, my eyes were opened on the sea. There, finning through the golden fronds that indeed wafted like locks of hair, I felt the beckoning of the underwater world. My response — the path I seek in my interactions with the ocean, in my diving, voyaging and writing — is to follow the Inuit shaman's example and comb the hair of the mother of the sea.

Further reading

Bradley, John, with Yanyuwa Families. *Singing Saltwater Country*. Allen & Unwin, 2010.

Branch, George. *Two Oceans: A Guide to the Marine Life of Southern Africa*. David Philip Publishers, 1994.

Cousteau, Jacques-Yves, with Frédéric Dumas. *The Silent World: A Story of Undersea Discovery and Adventure*. Harper & Brothers, 1953.

Cresswell, Tim. *Place: An Introduction*. Wiley-Blackwell, 2013.

Doak, Wade. *Sharks and Other Ancestors*. Hodder & Stoughton, 1975.

Graham, Mary. 'Some Thoughts about the Philosophical Underpinnings of Aboriginal Worldviews'. *Worldviews: Environment, Culture, Religion* 3 (1999): 105–18.

Grey, Zane. *Tales of the Angler's Eldorado, New Zealand*. Harper & Brothers, 1926.

Hau'ofa, Epeli. *We Are the Ocean*. University of Hawai'i Press, 2008.

Kimmerer, Robin Wall. *Braiding Sweetgrass*. Milkweed Editions, 2013.

Mallory, J. K. 'Abnormal Waves on the South-East of South Africa'. *International Hydrographic Review* 51 (1974): 89–129.

Mathews, Freya. *Reinhabiting Reality*. State University of New York Press, 2005.

Morton, John, and Michael Miller. *The New Zealand Seashore*. Collins, 1968.

Naidu, Vijay, Epeli Hau'ofa and Eric Waddell (eds). *A New Oceania: Rediscovering Our Sea of Islands*. University of the South Pacific, 1993.

New Zealand Waitangi Tribunal. *Ko Aotearoa Tēnei*. Legislation Direct, 2011.

Pelly, David F. *The Sacred Hunt*. University of Washington Press, 2001.

Smith, J. L. B. *The Sea Fishes of Southern Africa*. Central New Agency, 1949.

Steinbeck, John. *The Log from the Sea of Cortez*. Viking Press, 1951.

About
the author

KENNEDY WARNE IS THE founding editor of *New Zealand Geographic* and has written extensively for that magazine and for its American counterpart, *National Geographic*. He has written books about the world's disappearing mangrove forests (*Let Them Eat Shrimp*), on the Tūhoe iwi (*Tūhoe: Portrait of a Nation*) and on his first 20 years with *New Zealand Geographic* (*Roads Less Travelled*), as well as two children's books in collaboration with illustrator Heather Hunt (*The Cuckoo and the Warbler* and *It's My Egg: And You Can't Have It!*). In addition to writing, for the past 13 years he has been the outdoors correspondent for Radio New Zealand's weekday *Nine to Noon* programme, with a segment called 'Off the Beaten Track'.

What I did and did not have (Neruda), 2012, a collaborative
intaglio etching on paper by Niue-based artist John Pule and
Wellington-based artist, author and poet Gregory O'Brien

MASSEY
UNIVERSITY
PRESS

First published in 2023 by Massey University Press

Private Bag 102904, North Shore Mail Centre
Auckland 0745, New Zealand

www.masseypress.ac.nz

Design by Megan van Staden

Cover: Detail from *What I did and did not have (Neruda)*,
reproduced in full on page 239

Page 184: Teweiariki Teaero, extracted from 'Songs of Rising Isles'

A catalogue record for this book is available from
the National Library of New Zealand

Printed and bound in Singapore by Markono Print Media Pte Ltd

ISBN: 978-1-99-101644-7

eISBN: 978-1-99-101660-7

ARTS COUNCIL OF NEW ZEALAND TOI AOTEAROA

The assistance of Creative New Zealand is
gratefully acknowledged by the publisher